FishWorks
Seafood Café
Cookbook

Mitchell Tonks

Absolute Press

First published in Great Britain in 2001 by
Absolute Press
Scarborough House
29 James Street West
Bath BA1 2BT
Phone 44 (0) 1225 316013
Fax 44 (0) 1225 445836
E-mail info@absolutepress.co.uk
Website www.absolutepress.co.uk

Reprinted 2003, 2004

Author and Art Direction: Mitchell Tonks
Visualisation: Anne Chinca
Photography: Carlo Chinca
(except p28, courtesy of Martin Hobbs,
veterinary surgeon)

Editor: Jon Croft
Designer: Matt Inwood

A catalogue record of this book is available
from the British Library

ISBN 1 899791 04 3

Printed and bound in Italy by Printer Trento

Contents

Acknowledgments

SADIE, BEN, KITTY AND MUM

I would need another book to properly acknowledge all the help and support I've had. There are so many people who have helped and influenced me in my life and my cooking – to all those people a very big thank you.

To everyone at FishWorks, past and present, who have all believed in and made their mark on the restaurants and me.

I would like to mention in name those people in my professional life who helped me along: Gary Jones for encouraging me on from being a frustrated chef; Dickie who showed me how to eat more; Mike Cole for making me believe that all work is creative; Laura who first interpreted my scribbles; Richie Stewart for Chicago; Tony Yeadon, Richard Brereton, Bill and Tracy who made filming fun; Anita and Nick Hutchins and John Strike, who helped me when I started; Andy Bird, a great chef who first worked with me at the café and saw it grow; Phil Davies for being himself and bringing a great team to FishWorks; Derry Treanor for the 'leg up'; Trevor Dartford, Roger Murray-Leach, Roy Morris, Malcolm Pearce and Jean Pierre for their commitment and belief; Carlo and Anne for the great photos; Robert and Karen for being a huge support, an education and dear friends; Peter Green for taking me fishing; my publisher, Jon Croft, for his guidance; Matt Inwood, who designed the book, and the rest of the team at Absolute who made something of my manuscript; Mike Bridgeman and Adam Reynolds who were there from the start; Gary, Matthew and all the chefs at FishWorks who make it a pleasure – along with all the other staff, your commitment has been amazing; and lastly, each one of our customers who have supported and enjoyed coming to FishWorks.

Thank you.

FishWorks and the Seafood Cafés

The idea behind FishWorks and the Seafood Cafés was a simple one. The finest, freshest fish served over the counter or direct from the kitchen in relaxed surroundings by people with a passion and knowledge. It worked because it was all about the fish it was serving to its customers. So much of the praise and accolades we received were due to the simple cooking styles used and the kitchen's understanding of the produce. The fish spoke for itself. My team of waiters, managers and chefs were all enthused by the daily arrivals from the catch, some species that even they hadn't seen before. Our passion somehow brought us closer to our guests who would want to know about the boat – the 'Joanna C' – and which fish were arriving the next day. If they wanted something different, could we get it?

I often talked to them about the magic of the coastal fish markets, the expertise of the auctioneers, the wonders of the catch and the characters amongst the buyers. I even took a willing crowd up to Billingsgate one evening so they could experience that most famous market firsthand. It was on that trip that one of them, Roger Murray–Leach, an accomplished cook himself, decided fish was for him. After a successful career in films he took the plunge with me to open more restaurants built around a fish-market-styled operation. We would make it fascinating by having tables surrounding a fish counter where people could choose from the display, take advice from the chefs, buy and drink good wine and feel comfortable in an exciting environment. It would be a new experience for many.

We have just opened our third FishWorks and aim to make fish more accessible all over the country by continuing the profession of fishmongering and serving our customers with the best of the day's landings from the coast, either on the plate or to take home with a few herbs and a lemon and a bit of advice from the chef.

Perhaps most rewarding of all is to see children coming into FishWorks with amazed looks on their faces as they wonder at the live crabs, prawns and lobsters on display or peer anxiously at a 100 kilo tuna, three times the size of them. I hope we are helping to make fish fun.

A company dedicated to the enjoyment of seafood

Introduction

I got into being a fishmonger, and later a chef, for the love of it.

The opportunity to work with food and especially seafood held a special thrill for me. I had read about urchins, oysters, turbot, tuna and other species, but had hardly ever had the pleasure of seeing them, except on a visit to a fishing port or whilst travelling abroad or in the occasional good fishmonger's that I had come across.

So the approach was simple; to find out how and where to get the finest and freshest fish and then sell it on to my would-be customers, who I assumed would also want to get their hands on this stuff. So, armed with some wonderful experiences of eating seafood throughout my life, I opened the doors of the Fish Market in Bath. I soon found out that I shared something with my customers – a lack of knowledge. I, however, had a great advantage: I had the best fish I had ever seen coming in everyday and a network of wonderful people supplying me, from local salmon fishermen, young schoolboys bringing me buckets of crayfish and a particular fisherman, Nick Hutchins, in Dartmouth, who would phone me from the boat on the way home from sea and excitedly tell me what was flipping around on the deck! He would give me a price and we would strike a deal. I was, and still am, amazed at what arrives during the night, all packaged in crisp white boxes that carry a smell that is familiar to me but so far removed from what you would normally expect to experience in the middle of an inland city. Some mornings it was quite surreal; there I was miles from the coast and all I could hear were gulls and experience that familiar waft of the fresh smell of the sea. I would rip the lids off the boxes and, buried in diamond-like nuggets of ice, were huge turbot, glistening mackerel – that reminded me of my school holidays fishing in Cornwall – and pretty red mullet, as stiff as darts all with lovely clear eyes that almost looked back at me. There have also been live shrimps caught in the crab pots, leaping all over the shop that gave me one of the finest eating experiences I have had yet – but then I say that about every fish meal.

So with all this wonderful produce coming in and a limited knowledge of cooking, I decided that I would try to cook something different everyday. This changed the way I ate and cooked and I quickly knew that the best dishes were the simple ones, that fresh fish stands on its own, just simply grilled or roasted with a handful of flavour. A small fish for one or a larger one for four, a bowl of equally fresh green leaves and good olive oil and a squeeze of lemon was becoming the norm. I found I could sell fish by describing how a dish could be and how to cook it: for instance, all that needed doing for razor clams was to steam them open, sprinkle them with garlic and butter-soaked breadcrumbs and some fresh chopped parsley and then pop them for a minute or so under the grill; or perhaps how a steak of exotic blue marlin just seared on the grill with a crisp salty finish would eat well with a piquant caper and anchovy mayonnaise and make a perfect supper for our customers as they rushed in on their way home from work before we closed for the day. They became enthusiastic and many discovered how simple it was to appreciate good, fresh seafood. Some years later I was to take the big leap and open a café – and I stress *café* – simply laid tables above the shop, with me cooking unfussy, fresh fish as I had done at home for the previous five years. It worked, people loved it and it was great to see our customers taking pleasure in the sheer delight of the first native oysters of the year, the first chunk of wild salmon or a grilled sole drizzled with nut brown lemony butter, flecked with fresh herbs, and a glass of chilled wine. The Green Street Seafood Café in Bath, as it was known, is still my kind of restaurant: simple and fresh with the emphasis on the ingredients. Over the years, as we have built our team, I have worked with some wonderful people and chefs who have all shared in enjoying this simple accessible approach to cooking fish. The one thing we all agree on is that you can't be better than what you cook with. Now we are planning the opening of more restaurants and fish markets over the next two years, so everyone will be able to get the freshest fish and shellfish, go and talk to our chefs, and, of course, enjoy a great meal. The new restaurants and markets are called FishWorks – because we think it does. To date, there is a FishWorks in Bath, Bristol and the pretty town of Christchurch in Dorset

This book is a collection of recipes and experiences that I hope will help inspire and give you confidence when it comes to cooking fish. I will guide you through choosing, what to keep in your store cupboard, how to cook fish perfectly and show you how versatile fish can be. Having been a fishmonger I can also pass on a few tips, so your knowledge will be well grounded.

Read the introduction to each recipe, let the recipe suit your occasion or mood and if you want to play around with it a bit, then do so. I have put lots of other suggestions alongside many of the recipes to encourage you to add your own ideas. Relax and have fun with the recipes. Just think, once you start there are literally hundreds of species available in the United Kingdom. You could spend a lifetime enjoying seeking them out and then taking a simple approach to cooking and enjoying the individuality and merits of each one.

There is only one rule – find the freshest produce you can and let it speak for itself. The other flavours added only seek to complement – the main star is the fish.

Cooking and Me

I was born in 1966 in Weston-super-Mare and spent my first 24 years by the sea.
I sailed on it, skied on it and fished in it. Fish and fisherman were a natural part of my life.
Both my grandmother and mother were great home cooks and from an early age I was
fascinated by the mysterious rituals that went on in the kitchen. They encouraged me to
be enquiring about food and to appreciate it, to learn how to eat and to realise that food
was meant to be fun.

It wasn't until I had decided on a radical change in my career that I began to reflect on
those times in my mother's kitchen and the fun that it had generated. I had decided to become
a fishmonger. Looking back it seems a crazy decision to have made in many ways – nothing
could have been further removed from my previous career, but I had grown frustrated.
I thought it terrible that a city like Bath, where I was living, couldn't provide its own people with
decent fish. I spent some months travelling up and down to Cornwall, establishing contacts
and getting a feel for the business. I realised that I loved everything to do with the business of
fish – the people, the produce and the enthusiastic consumers. Amongst the many wonderful
people that I met was Robert Wing of Wing of St Mawes who was to become our major
supplier of fish. Robert is committed to sourcing and supplying the very finest fish and it is
dedication like his that enables us all to appreciate the best seafood around.

My move from behind the counter to the heat of the kitchen at FishWorks was a quick one.
I had begun to experiment at home with various recipes for the many species that we sold
and started a seafood cookery school for cutomers in the shop in a very quiet way. With my
confidence further enhanced I took the big step of opening the café upstairs. It proved to
be a hit almost immediately and I was soon having to catch up with the demands of a
professional kitchen. To date the Seafood Café has been praised for its fresh simple approach
to cooking and with the benefit of our success in Bath we have begun to open new FishWorks
around the country.

I still run the FishWorks cookery school and will soon begin cookery classes for children.
I hope you can see that even from a home cook's background anything is possible and that
this book will inspire you to cook more fish.

FishWorks
Seafood Café
Cookbook

The Essentials

Getting Started

Before using this book take a bit of time to read through the chapters in this Essentials section. It will help you to understand my approach to eating and cooking fish. You will notice as you flick through the recipes that a number of them have the FishWorks logo at the top of the page (as illustrated above). These are the recipes that have become our FishWorks Classics and are served regularly in all our restaurants.

Fish cookery isn't hard, it just requires some basic knowledge and a good supply of fresh fish. So seek out your nearest fishmonger and make him your friend. Log onto FishWorks.co.uk for a list of the best and where to find them. *Rick Stein's Seafood Lover's Guide* is also an excellent and well-researched resource. I have listed my favourite food suppliers on page 23. You can, of course, order your fish direct from the purchases at Newlyn fish market using Wing of St Mawes' retail mail order service. Details of this service can also be found on page 23.

There are no special tools or ingredients that you absolutely must have to cook fish, but I have listed my basic store cupboard that never lets me down on page 21. There is nothing amazing about it and much of it you will probably already have hiding in the dark recesses of your larder. On page 22 I have listed my favourite bits of kit which, through experience, I have learnt give me the best results with the minimum of effort.

I would also recommend that you go out and buy a good fish cookery reference book that covers species of fish in rather greater detail than I do in this recipe book. I recommend and regularly refer to Alan Davidson's *Mediterranean Seafood* and Jane Grigson's *Fish Book*. They are like old friends to me, they are always there and never let me down.

So, find a good fishmonger and support him, establish a store cupboard and equip yourself with a few basic bits of kit and splash out on a good fish reference book to complement this one. Having done that you will be ready to get cooking and begin a fantastic culinary voyage of discovery.

Buying Policy

In order to get the very best out of your fish cooking with fish you will need to adopt one golden rule – only buy the freshest produce available. Far better to buy spanking fresh fish and cook it simply with just the addition of a few fresh herbs and a squeeze of lemon juice than to labour for hours over a complicated sauce to marry with a tired and past-it apology for a fish.

Fresh fish is easy to recognise. It should look as if it has just come out of the sea. It should glisten, look almost alive with its eyes clear and bright and ready to wink back at you. Fresh fish smells of the sea. Don't be afraid to prod it, it should be firm to the touch. Beware of fish counters displaying headless fish, they probably have something to hide. A strong smell in a shop probably means go somewhere else! Try to avoid going out to shop with a preconceived idea of what you want. Be flexible and buy the best fish on the counter and not that tired old turbot in the corner which you had originally planned to cook.

I know, I know – good fish isn't cheap. There are, however, some species, such as grey mullet, mackerel, gurnard, pollack and cuttlefish that are always a bargain and are superb to eat. No one should object to paying a fair price for a really fresh fish. While we sleep, work goes on to ensure that the day's catch gets to us. By seeking out the freshest fish and demanding the very best of you fishmonger you will help keep the whole industry afloat. Buying well today will ensure fish for tomorrow.

One of the most common questions that I am asked as a fishmonger and chef is, 'How much fish will I need?' The answer varies with each species as different fish yield different amounts of flesh. The portion size you should look for is about 150-175g/5-6oz. The simple chart below will help you decide how much fish you will need for an average main course. This is only a guideline though, and appetite, as always, will have the last say.

Fish type	Yield of flesh	Amount per person
Any fish fillet, including, tuna, swordfish or other game fish	100%	150-175g/5-6oz
Plaice, lemon sole, turbot and other flat fish	50%	350g/12oz
Salmon, bass, mackerel and all other round fish	70%	275g/9oz

Storing Fish

The storing of fish is always an issue of concern to people. In an ideal world you would have caught your fresh and flapping fish yourself and simply grilled it over a wood fire on the beach at sunset. Sadly, this is not the way most of us are able to enjoy fish.

Fresh fish will last for up to twelve days out of water. For this to happen the storage requires special attention. The fish should be chilled at no more and no less than zero degrees Celsius and be covered in lots of ice, which will help wash away any bacteria that might build up. As temperatures rise during the summer months though, and the decks of boats warm up, so the shelf life of the fish will be shortened. A boat that has been at sea for a few days in hot temperatures but has not stored its catch in appropriate conditions will not be landing fresh fish. So, when your fishmonger tells you with great pride that the fish looking back at you with tired eyes 'came in this morning' it is no guarantee of its freshness. Once again, the importance of recognising fresh fish and having a fishmonger that you can trust is paramount.

Once you have found your fresh fish and taken it home you should immediately put it on a plate and cover it with parchment paper or a damp cloth and put it in the coldest part of the fridge. If it is in prime condition it should keep for up to two days. Ideally you should buy fish for that same day's consumption, but a Saturday purchase for a Sunday fish feast is fine. Avoid fish on Monday as coastal markets don't operate until early on Monday which means that fishmongers and restaurants will not be getting fresh supplies until Tuesday. This rule does not apply if you live on, or very close to, the coast as supplies there are more immediate and tend to be same-day.

Preparing to Cook

Most of the recipes that feature in this book require that the fish be cooked very quickly. In order to make the experience at the stove enjoyable and seamless I would encourage you to take some tips from a professional kitchen:

Have all your ingredients prepared in advance. This is always done with a glass of wine close to hand. Cooking is meant to be fun.

Everything that should be sliced and chopped, should be sliced and chopped, whilst sauces and dressings that can be made in advance, should be made in advance,

Have your cooker or grill pre-heated and ready to go.

Don't be afraid to taste the dish as you go along and allow your taste to lead you. You will soon develop a feel for the way flavours and recipes develop. Neil Perry, from the outstanding Sydney restaurant Rockpool, writes on the subject in his wonderful book of the same name; 'Make sure the flavours are always in harmony: no single flavour should ever be dominant. It can be the most predominant, but it should not be at the expense of balance.'

Simplicity should be your watchword. Just the fish and a single accompaniment or pre-prepared sauce can be all that is needed. I have given some brilliant accompaniments and sauces in sections of this book, which we use all the time at our Seafood Cafés.

The Cooking

On countless occasions I have been asked by worried customers how long they should cook fish and how they will know when it is done. It is difficult to give a precise answer as individual ovens vary in temperature. There are also differences between gas and electric cookers and don't even get me started on the subject of Agas. Only you know your kitchen and your cooker.

I firmly believe that if you understand the nature of what you are cooking then the chances are you will get it right. Try not to think of fish as simply meat from the sea. The various different types of cooking methods required for different types of meat cannot be translated to the cooking of fish. The job of the oven, and I invariably use an oven, is to finish the fish and 'set' it. Try to imagine the oven as an instrument that can provide just enough all round heat to firm up the wobbly feel of the fish, rather than as a tool to tenderise and cook. Think this way and you will find yourself checking in the oven every so often waiting for that firmness to be realised. Soon your technique will be perfection delivered by experience. Shellfish, of course, demand a different technique and this is covered in recipes later in the book.

The Pan-roasting Method

The pan-roasting method is my key to success for the fish cook. The principle behind this cooking method ensures that your fish will both look and taste great. Cook the fish first in the pan – you want it crisp and golden. I never use butter for frying as I think it has a tendency to burn and taint the flavour of the fish. I prefer a good quality vegetable oil. First, I get a non-stick pan, add some oil and heat it for a minute or two to get it up to cooking speed. When the oil is hot, I lightly season the fish and cook it for two to three minutes, turning it once. This will be the side you see on the plate and will be crisp and golden. Providing the pan has a metal handle, not a plastic one, I then transfer it to the oven (for plastic, simply transfer the fish to a roasting tray). The oven should be at maximum temperature. Check the fish every few minutes; touch it; you are waiting for it to 'set'. If you are cooking a whole fish don't worry about pulling back a bit of skin to check the progress. Soon you will instinctively know when your fish is cooked. This is the pan-roasting method and it will work for you every time and will produce the most wonderful and succulent fish. If you are grilling fish, start it under the grill then finish it in the oven, 20 minutes is about right for a 450g/1lb fish.

The Store Cupboard

The list below represents my basic store cupboard.

There are plenty more ingredients I could list but these will form a basic selection from which a whole range of dishes can be created. As you build up your confidence and understanding you will add to your store cupboard, reflecting your own personal preferences.

Apply the same buying policy to your fresh ingredients as you do to your fish. Buy the freshest; this will give you the best flavour. Keep trying new things. I always have chervil in the store, not only does it taste great but a few sprigs of this pretty herb on the plate, or mixed in with a salad garnish, can give a really professional looking finish. If you have an Asian supermarket near you, use it – they are like an Aladdin's cave. Stock up on sour yellow curry paste, fresh lemongrass and galangal and try 'Ikan Bilis', tiny dried anchovies which are wonderful deep-fried and sprinkled over a bowl of noodles or salad, or do as I do, and eat them like peanuts!

Ginger

Sea salt

Garlic

Fresh herbs – tarragon, chervil, coriander, parsley, dill, rosemary, thyme (try and buy cut herbs and store them in the fridge in a plastic container covered with a damp cloth)

Dried bay leaves

Good quality saffron

Fennel bulbs

Star anise

Fresh chillies

Dried chilli flakes

Peppers

Tomatoes

Lemons

Limes

Unsalted butter

Good olive oil (splash out on a bottle of good stuff – I like a brand called Ravida – or have a good quality lemon oil on hand)

An ordinary virgin olive oil, for dressings

Vegetable oil

A bottle of pastis or Pernod (maybe that bottle of ouzo you bought on holiday could have a use!)

White wine

White wine vinegar

Red wine vinegar

Salted capers

Salted anchovies

Fish stock (I make it fresh and then freeze it in containers)

Dried pasta and noodles

Favourite Bits of Kit

These are my very basic, favourite and essential bits of kit that I would recommend to all would–be fish cooks to invest in. Of course, as you discover different types of fish and different recipes you will probably want to expand your selection of utensils. I have listed some suppliers at the foot of this page.

Global cook's knife – sharp!
Grillplate – essential; try to get one with thin ridges
Hand processor with attachments
Non-stick frying pan
Copper sauté pan with high sides for cooking and serving stews
Flat metal roasting trays – great for popping under the grill
A good fish slice with a short handle
Palette knife – for turning fish fillets and scallops
A big pan with a lid for steaming shellfish
Oyster knife – pointed one preferably
Tongs
A barbecue – for outside the kitchen door!
Small plastic bottles for oils or dressing, with pointed pouring spouts which can be cut to suit the flow

Baristas Supply Co.
Unit 5, Gatton Road, St Werburghs
Bristol BS2 9TF
T 0117 9540300 **F** 0117 9540400

One of the best and most competitive suppliers for all of the above.

Kitchens

4-5 Queen Street, Bath BA1 2JS
T 01225 330524 **F** 01225 481676
167 Whiteladies Road, Bristol BS8 2SQ
T 0117 9739614 **F** 0117 9238565
14 High Street, Cardiff CF10 1AX
T 0292 0229814 **F** 0292 0222788

Another good, dependable supplier of essential kitchen equipment.

Food Suppliers That I Recommend

**Fishworks Seafod Café
& Traditional Fishmongers**
E enquire@fishworks.co.uk
W www.fishworks.co.uk

6 Green Street, Bath BA1 2JY
T 01225 447794 **F** 01225 447562
128 Whiteladies Road, Bristol BS8 2RS
T 0117 9741950 **F** 0117 9744933
10 Church Street, Christchurch BH231BW
T 01202 487000 **F** 01202 487001
**6 Turnham Green Terrace, Chiswick,
London W4 1QP**
T 0208 994 0086 **F** 0208 994 0778

Williams Kitchen Ltd
3 Fountain Street, Nailsworth,
Gloucestershire GL6 0BL
T 01453 832240 **F** 01453 835950
E food@williamskitchen.co.uk
W www.williamskitchen.co.uk
A great little delicatessen selling allsorts
with a first-rate fish counter and service.

Ashtons
Ashton House, 72-74 City Road,
Cardiff CF24 3DD **T** 0292 0480244
A good traditional fishmongers with a huge
slab which means a great variety. It gets really
busy so the fish turns over and is always in
spanking fresh condition.

Teohs
26-34 Lower Ashley Road, St Agnes
Bristol BS2 9NP
T 0117 907 1191 **F** 0117 9071193
A brilliant Chinese supermarket. Great
people who know their stuff. Stock up
on everything and have lunch inside where
they have a great traditional Chinese menu.
A really good way to spend a morning.

Steve Hatt
88-90 Essex Road, Islington
London N1 8LU **T** & **F** 0207 2263963
Famed for years, a good traditional shop
that impresses me every time I visit. He has
a good range, including exotic species.

Britannia Shellfish Ltd
The Viviers, Beesands, Kingsbridge
Devon TQ7 2EH **T** & **F** 01548 581186
This is my favourite and the fish couldn't
be fresher. It is run by my friends Nick and
Anita Hutchins who send some fish to us.
Nick fishes everyday from his boat moored
outside their house on the beach and returns
home at night with the finest Start Bay crab
and lobster. He also has fish landed each
day by his family. Great fish, great people
and definitely worth a trip.

Wing of St Mawes
4 Warren Road,
Indian Queens Industrial Estate,
Indian Queens, Cornwall TR9 6TL
T 01726 861666 **F** 01726 861668
E admin@cornish-seafood.co.uk
W www.cornish-seafood.co.uk

This is our main source of supply and
Robert gets the best fish from the daily
auctions at Newlyn as well as local boats.
Each day there are over 40 species
available, depending on the weather.
The same superb fish that we use in our
restaurants is now available not only from
our fishmongers' counters at FishWorks but
can also be sent direct from the quayside
to arrive the next day. For a brochure visit
www.FishWorks.co.uk and leave your details.

The Future for Fish

It is always talked about – are we over-fishing? Is supply for the recent new interest in fish going to be sustained? I am a fishmonger and chef and obviously care about these issues. As a company, FishWorks cares. We constantly seek and demand those species which are from sustainable fishing grounds and not mass-trawled by factory ships. We also support aquaculture or fish farming as there are certain species which farm extremely well: sea bass, for instance – now in great demand and if it wasn't for farmed bass we would now be putting huge pressure on wild stocks. When we are affecting and influencing nature what we do needs to be policed – in this case to ensure the future for fish. Robert Wing, my friend, and our fish supplier in Cornwall, is an expert on this subject. He has been in and around the industry for most of his life and still runs a fishing boat, so these issues are close to his heart. I have taken his view and advice here and it is encouraging to learn from someone so close to the bottom of our supply chain.

Clearly, the common fisheries policy has failed both fish and fishermen. Clearly, there is no simple answer, otherwise it would have been implemented a long time ago. There are many uncontrollable variables – certain types of trawling for certain species have an effect on the habitat of others, the sea is deep and fishing is not selective, fishermen cannot choose what goes into their trawl or visibly pick out small fish from mature. Scallop dredgers don't catch fish but harm their feeding grounds in search of their catch, but then if we relied on diver caught scallops all the time the price would be prohibitive and that market would die and maybe never be fished again. So what can be done? There are solutions and people, governments and organisations around the world are actively trying to control the problem to secure the future of our seas and fish stocks. Fishermen are aware of the problems and are doing their bit to co-operate. On my visits to Newlyn I see biologists working on the market, ageing fish to ensure proper policing of the stocks in various areas: so things are happening.

I believe we will control this problem in time. What we can do is to demand our fish be caught by ethical methods. To stop buying fish wouldn't be the answer, as there is always a market somewhere. And without a home market there will be little funds to go back into control. Perhaps by eating more we can become more aware. It is better to have a fishing ground with a fleet which is managed than unmanaged seas left open for careless exploitation.

Myself and everyone at FishWorks will be co-operating to secure tomorrow's catches.

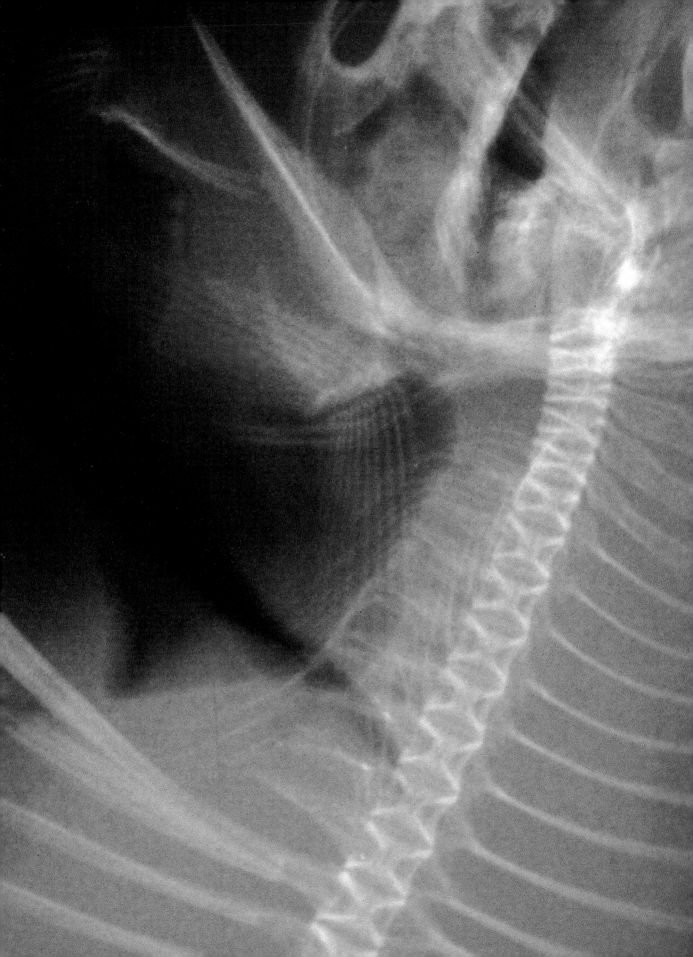

FishWorks
Seafood Café
Cookbook

Basic Sauces

The sauces, butters and dressings that follow here are ones that have become my personal favourites over the years. They never let me down and never get boring. Every fish has its own flavour and qualities and these sauces help bring them out. Many of the sauces here can be regarded as a base from which you add different flavours to suit your mood. For instance, I use a classic white sauce and often add parsley to it to make wonderful parsley sauce. You could just as easily add tarragon and the same sauce base would become tarragon sauce, add a squeeze of lemon and it becomes tarragon and lemon sauce.

Be open-mined, keep it simple and be flexible. Cooking fish is about being in touch with the ingredients and not being a slave to a set of rules.

Good Garlic Butter

I make this in quantity and then roll it into sausages in Clingfilm and then freeze it. When I need some I just cut a bit off – it's always there.

8 cloves of plump garlic
2 handfuls of curly parsley, chopped
Handful of tarragon, chopped

Good pinch of sea salt
Dash of Pernod
450g/1lb unsalted butter, softened

Place all the ingredients except the butter into a food processor and blend to a smooth paste. In a bowl mix the paste thoroughly and evenly with a wooden spoon into the butter. Roll into a sausage in Clingfilm, freeze and use as required.

I use this a lot for brushing onto grilled fish, tossing spinach in with a handful of pine nuts and tossing green beans in with a handful of shallots. I always finish it with a squeeze of lemon and a pinch of sea salt to sharpen it up.

Rosemary and Anchovy Butter

A great back-up as a tasty sauce for that last minute bit of prime fish you spotted on the way home. Make it and store it in the same way as garlic butter. Melt it in a pan, add some chopped tomato flesh, a handful of chopped parsley, a squeeze of lemon and pour it over.

½ a jar of salted anchovy fillets with the oil
2 cloves of garlic
2 sprigs of rosemary (pick the leaves off

and discard the branch)
450g/1lb unsalted butter

Put the anchovies, with their oil into a processor with the garlic and rosemary. Blend until smooth and stir into the softened butter.

Fish Stock

Fish stock is so easy to make and there are only a few rules to follow. I find it easier to make it in batches and then freeze it in small containers – it is always there for you when you need it. It's good to have days making basics and nothing else. Crack a bottle of wine, read a few cookbooks while you're waiting and you can ensure that the kitchen is then ready for anything.

Fish stock is a carrier of flavour it is not a sauce on it's own so don't expect it to taste delicious. The best bones to use are turbot, brill, monkfish and sole bones. Avoid salmon, trout and sea bass as they can make the stock chalky.

1 leek, chopped
1/2 onion, chopped
2 carrots, chopped
1 stick of celery, chopped
1 fennel bulb, chopped

Few sprigs of thyme
1kg cleaned fish bones – (your fishmonger will give them to you free)
Glass of white wine

Sweat the vegetables and herbs in a little olive oil until softened. Break up the bones into chunks, so they fit in the pan, and give it a good stir. Add the wine then enough water to cover. Gently simmer for 40 minutes skimming any froth from the top with a spoon. Strain and then return to the pan and boil to reduce by a third. This is the process where water will evaporate and intensify the flavour. Just keep it gently boiling until a third of it is gone.

Makes 2 pints / 1.2 litres

Fresh Herb, Tomato and Grilled Artichoke Dressing

Olive oil-based sauces are easy to knock up in a hurry, they taste great and are healthy. Because they are made at the last minute they are really fresh tasting and suitable for any fish and shellfish. Avoid using them with oily fish such as mackerel or herrings.

125ml/¼ pint good olive oil
Pinch coriander seeds
Small clove of garlic, pasted (see page 41)
1 grilled artichoke heart, roughly chopped
1 ripe tomato, inside removed and flesh
  chopped

Few basil leaves, shredded
Few tarragon leaves, shredded
Few mint leaves, shredded
Pinch of sea salt
Juice of ½ lemon

Warm the olive oil, coriander seeds and garlic and leave to infuse for 10 minutes. Add the remaining ingredients with lemon juice added last. Spoon over your fish.

Serves 2

Olive Rillettes

The very Mediterranean flavour of these olive rillettes works well with small grilled red mullet. It can also be spread onto grilled bread or served in ramekin dishes as a starter surrounded by a pile of marinated anchovies. Poached fish can benefit from a light saucing as can vegetables, mashed potato or polenta.

150g/5oz unsalted butter
2 sprigs fresh thyme, picked
Good pinch dried oregano
½ handful chopped parsley

150g/5oz stoned black olives, finely chopped
Few turns of black pepper
Squeeze lemon juice

Gently melt the butter, add the herbs then the olives and lastly the black pepper and lemon juice. Put into ramekins and allow to set in the fridge. Spread on fresh bread and eat with your fish.

Serves 6

Try this too...

Melt some olive butter add some chopped tomato and basil and use it as a quick sauce.

Salsa Verde

This is a fragrant mixture of fresh garden herbs and is a great way to reap the harvest of the kitchen window boxes. At the restaurants we leave it on the tables for guests to dip their bread in. We are constantly asked for the recipe, so here it is. Make it in advance but add the lemon juice before serving, as it will discolour the fresh herbs if added sooner. I add a chopped boiled egg to it sometimes, I love them, but it won't spoil it if you don't put one in.

Handful of tarragon
1½ handfuls of fresh parsley
Handful of fresh mint
Handful of fresh basil
1 clove of garlic

4 anchovy fillets
1 tbsp capers
250ml/8fl oz good first pressed olive oil
Juice of 1 lemon

Put everything, except the lemon juice, in the food processor with a little of the olive oil and whizz to a coarse paste. Stir in the rest of the olive oil and spoon over your dish or put into a dipping bowl to eat with bread.

Serves 8

Salsa Rossa

This is the red version. I love it and there is nothing that it doesn't work with. It's worth keeping the base to it in the fridge. Just add the herbs and lemon juice at the last minute and serve a spoonful with anything off the grill – it's colourful, and as versatile as that.

1 clove of garlic, pasted (see page 41)
1 red pepper, roasted, peeled and chopped
  into small dice
2 leaves of radicchio, shredded
Handful of fresh basil, chopped
Handful of fresh mint, chopped
1 tsp capers

1 small chilli, deseeded and finely chopped
2 anchovy fillets, roughly chopped
1 tomato, deseeded and chopped into
  small dice
Juice of 1 lemon
Pinch of sea salt

Mix it all together, add a squeeze of lemon juice and a pinch of crunchy sea salt.

Serves 4

Hollandaise Sauce

This is all butter and quite rich but it's luxurious and can be knocked up in seconds. Traditionally, it is made in a bowl over steaming water. I have learnt to hold the bowl just above the heat whilst whisking, taking it away occasionally so as not to allow too much heat near the eggs. It works and saves having to boil a pan of water each time. Often I substitute the plain butter for garlic and then spoon it over the fish and pop it under a hot grill for a few seconds. It glazes with a light brown crust concealing the fish underneath, giving it a very tempting appearance.

2 egg yolks
1 tbsp cold water
200g/7oz unsalted butter, melted

Juice of 1 lemon
Salt and pepper for seasoning

Put the eggs and water into a bowl and whisk over a medium heat until it doubles in size and thickens – it does this because the eggs are cooking, do it for too long and you have scrambled eggs, so go easy.

Remove from the heat and in a gentle stream pour in the butter whilst whisking. The sauce will thicken further. Add the lemon juice and seasoning. It should taste quite lemony and clean, the lemon juice just cutting through the butter.

Serves 4, easily

Try this too...

Steam open a few clams and mussels in water with a pinch of saffron. Remove them from their shells and add to some Hollandaise sauce. Reduce the pan juices and stir them in. Add a handful of chopped tarragon. Pour over a piece of cooked fish and pop under the grill to glaze them – it's great.

Béchamel Sauce

Most cookbooks have a recipe for this. Mine isn't any different. The classic way works best and there is no point in trying to change something which has been used successfully and enjoyed for years by many.

½ onion	8 peppercorns
2 bay leaves	Pinch of salt
4 cloves	50g/2oz butter
300ml/10fl oz milk	1 tbsp flour

Make two cuts in the onion and put the bay leaves into them. Push the cloves into the onion. Place this in a pan with the milk, the peppercorns and the salt, bring to the boil and gently simmer for 5 minutes. Leave to infuse for 20 minutes. In a separate pan melt the butter and add the flour to make a smooth paste or *roux*, as it is called. Remove the onion from the milk and whilst off the heat, whisk the milk gradually into the butter and flour paste – a little at a time is best. Return it to the heat to allow it to thicken and cook out the flour. If it is too thick add a little more milk. The consistency should be like velvety double cream. Store this in the fridge and use it when needed.

Serves 4

Green Basil Pesto

This is a classic dish and can be made in advance. It can be stored in the fridge, in a sealed jar with a layer of olive oil on top. It is delicious and summery whether stirred into pasta as an accompaniment or used as a dressing for roasted vegetables.

1 large bunch green basil, stalks removed	25g/1oz Parmesan shavings
1 clove of garlic	100ml/3fl oz good olive oil
1 tbsp pine nuts	Sea salt to taste

Put all the ingredients into a food processor and pulse until you have a coarse creamy paste. Add salt to your taste.

Mayonnaise

Homemade mayonnaise is delicious. Made thick and creamy with the addition of a few herbs it can make the perfect accompaniment to freshly boiled shellfish. Add chopped capers and gherkins for a Tartare sauce, which is great with fishcakes and fried fish. Make it in advance as it will keep for a few days in the fridge.

2 egg yolks
1 tsp Dijon mustard
1 tsp white wine vinegar
75ml/3fl oz plain oil such as vegetable

75ml/3fl oz olive oil
Salt and pepper
Juice of 1/2 lemon

Put the egg yolks in a bowl with the mustard and vinegar. Mix the oils together and pour onto the egg yolks in a steady stream whilst whisking until you have a thick creamy mayonnaise. Lastly, season and add the lemon juice.

Serves 4

Try this too...

Add any chopped fresh herb to the mayonnaise or add chilli, fish sauce, holy basil or coriander and lime juice for a Thai flavour or just stir a spoonful of mild curry paste into it and serve with a chunk of smoked haddock.

Aioli

Rich mayonnaise made with thick green olive oil, heavily flavoured with garlic. It is perfect on a croûton to top Zuppa De Pescatore (see page 158) or other fish stews. And I always have a bowl on the table when eating steamed clams or mussels. Crisp-fried goujons of sole also benefit from being dunked in aioli.

2 egg yolks
1 tsp Dijon mustard
4 cloves of garlic, pasted (see page 41)

150ml/5fl oz good olive oil
Juice of 1/2 lemon
Sea salt

Put the egg yolks in a bowl with the mustard and garlic. Whilst whisking add the olive oil in a steady stream until a thick emulsion is formed. Add the lemon juice, season, and let it stand for an hour before serving.

Serves 4

FishWorks
Seafood Café
Cookbook

Accompaniments

The accompaniments that follow in this section are the same as those you would find at our restaurants. They are simple and full of flavour and act as a wonderful foil to the fish dishes we cook. This whole book is about simplicity and I don't intend to get complicated now.

The recipes that follow in this section are easy and fun to make, are bursting with great flavours and glow with vibrant colour. A perfectly grilled piece of fish, sprinkled with salt and a squeeze of lemon sitting on a plain white plate accompanied by a stunning side dish can reach perfection.

Rosemary and Anchovy Potatoes with Garlic

These are similar to the classic French dauphinois style. I like them on their own as a simple baked potato supper served with salad or a bowl of fresh peas. They are great served with John Dory or chargrilled monkfish fillets, but you can try them with anything.

8 anchovy fillets, salted ones in oil, finely
   chopped, reserving the oil
2 cloves of garlic, pasted (see method below)
570ml/1 pint double cream
2 sprigs of rosemary

25g/1oz butter
4 medium-sized potatoes, peeled and very finely
   sliced, preferably on a mandolin
2 tbsp Parmesan, finely grated
Salt and pepper

In the reserved anchovy oil sweat the garlic and half the anchovies until softened and melted. Pour in the cream and add a sprig of rosemary then bring to a gentle simmer. Take off the heat and leave to infuse for five minutes.

Lightly butter a roasting dish and layer the potatoes with the remaining anchovies and the rosemary. Remove the rosemary from the cream and pour over to cover the potatoes. Sprinkle with Parmesan and bake in a hot oven until cooked – about 40 minutes. They are cooked when soft inside with a crisp golden brown crust outside. If you want to show off then cut them out of the baking dish with a round pastry cutter and top with a handful of small, dressed salad leaves.

Serves 4

Pasting garlic

I use garlic a lot in my cookery. You can easily control the flavour of this pungent vegetable: if you want a mild flavour, slice it, the finer you go the stronger it will get. I like to paste my garlic and let it flavour the initial oils I add to the cooking pans. I do this by hand and never use a garlic press. Elizabeth David devotes a whole page entitled 'Garlic Presses are Useless' in *Is There a Nutmeg in the House?* I think she's right.

To paste the garlic put the clove onto a chopping board, place a heavy knife on its side on top of it, and give it a thump with your hand. Sprinkle it with salt and then, with the knife, gradually rub the blade across it pushing down and working the salt in – the salt acts as an abrasive. You will have perfect garlic paste and no garlic press to pick clean!

Buttered Jersey Royals with Fresh Mint

One of the highlights of the year. Other new potatoes are also good especially Cypriot or Cornish, in any case all must be as freshly dug as possible. I'm not going to tell you how to boil potatoes but the best way I have found for getting the flavour of mint into them is to use as fresh a herb as possible, pick off the leaves and boil the potatoes with a little salt and the stems of the mint. When they are cooked toss them in butter and sprinkle with chopped mint leaves.

Roasted New Potatoes with Rosemary and Sea Salt

Bundle the new potatoes onto a roasting tray with the rosemary, sprinkle with sea salt and drizzle olive oil over. Shake the tray until they are well coated and roast for 20-30 minutes in a hot oven. Toss in butter just before serving.

Try this too...

For added luxury cook the potatoes as above. Just before serving make a cross cut on the top of each one. With your fingers squeeze the potato until the inside oozes from the cut, top with a teaspoon of *crème fraîche*, a few chopped chives and lastly a teaspoon of the best caviar you can afford!

Fennel, Mint, Coriander and Chilli Salad

Fennel has a natural affinity with fish, as does anything with that lovely aniseedy twang. A handful of tarragon in a sauce or salad or a glug of Pernod or other anise flavoured alcohol can give a real edge. Just the addition of fresh herbs and lemon juice brings out the best in this wonderful salad. Great with a few seared scallops or a piece of grilled oily fresh mackerel.

1 fennel bulb – buy one with a nice fluffy top
1/2 handful fresh mint, chopped
1 mild chilli, finely chopped
Pinch of sea salt

1/2 handful fresh coriander, chopped
Juice of 1 lemon
Good olive oil

Pick the fronds off the fennel and put into a bowl with the mint and chilli. Very finely slice the fennel, this is best done on a mandolin, and add to the bowl with the other ingredients. Toss together with the lemon juice and olive oil and serve.

Serves 4

Side Caesar Salad

Caesar salad makes a great lunch on its own but can make a good side dish with almost any fish. Follow the recipe on page 166 but just make it smaller!

Oven-roast Tomatoes with Pesto

These have been on our menu ever since we opened and are similar to sun-dried tomatoes except they are cooked instead of being dried out in the sun. They can be made in advance and kept in a kilner jar in the fridge and used in salads or just quickly fried in the pan with a little Worcestershire sauce and eaten on toast with eggs and bacon in the morning. You could even chop them up with a few black olives tossed in pasta for a quick supper. They are also excellent as an accompaniment to grilled fish and shellfish. I am told that they also work extremely well in an Aga. My Australian friends, and great cooks, Chris and Lizzie who run the Vobster Inn in Somerset, cook them overnight in their Aga. Chris calls them Moon-Dried Tomatoes.

Make as many as you'd like in one batch and I'd encourage you to make as big a batch as possible as they're a welcome accompaniment to the store cupboard.

For the pesto

Two handfuls of purple or green basil leaves, or a mix of both

1 tbsp pine nuts

1 clove of garlic

570ml/1 pint good olive oil

1 tbsp Parmesan, freshly grated

Good ripe plum tomatoes (I serve 2 tomatoes as a side dish)

Handful of fresh tarragon

1 tsp sea salt

275ml/8fl oz of good olive oil

Ground black pepper

First make the pesto by placing all the ingredients in a food processor and blitzing together. Place in the fridge until needed. You may find that overnight it will set. Don't worry, it hasn't spoiled and will just need to be removed from the fridge and allowed to breathe at room temperature for an hour or so for the oil to 'melt'.

Cut the tomatoes in half, lay them on a roasting tray, sprinkle the tarragon and sea salt over along with a dash of olive oil and pop them in the bottom of your oven for a minimum of 5-6 hours or in an Aga in the cool part of the oven overnight. Remove them from the oven. They should be shrivelled but still juicy. If you find they are blackened, or look almost grilled around the edges, then you have had the oven too hot. You must leave it low, be patient and do not worry, you will not start a fire!

To serve, place both halves on a side plate and drizzle pesto over the top. You can, if you like, add a small handful of salad leaves to garnish.

Spinach with Garlic and Pine Nuts

This is a favourite way of cooking spinach. Spot on as a side dish but also good as a colourful bed for fish in the middle of a white plate with a sauce poured around. You could also add a pinch of chilli flakes or a tablespoon of juicy fat raisins, or both.

25g/1oz garlic butter (see page 31)
1/2 tbsp pine nuts
Allow 175g/6oz washed and picked spinach

per person
1 tbsp water
Sea salt

Melt the garlic butter gently in a pan and when melted and foaming add the pine nuts and cook for a minute or so. Add the spinach and the water. Give it a stir to make sure the spinach is well coated and continue to cook over a gentle heat until just wilted. Season with sea salt.

Serves 1

Green Beans with Shallots and Garlic

If you can, use a mix of green beans and English new season's runner beans.

4 handfuls of beans, green beans trimmed at
   the ends and runner beans, sliced
20g/1oz butter

1 clove of garlic, pasted
1 shallot, finely chopped
Sea salt

Cook the beans in salted water until *al dente* then refresh in ice-cold water which will stop them cooking and help keep their colour. To serve, gently melt the butter in a fireproof serving dish and add the garlic and shallots. When they have softened add the beans and heat through gently, tossing all the time. Season with sea salt and serve.

Serves 4

Marinated Red Peppers with Lemon Oil and Thyme

Sweet-roasted peppers served at room temperature make a great accompaniment to a piece of grilled or roasted fish. They can be marinated in any combination of herbs and garlic but try not to use soft herbs like basil and chives, instead stick to harder herbs like rosemary, oregano, marjoram or thyme. Also try adding garlic. Once they are made they will keep for up to a week. When all the peppers have been gobbled up be sure to keep the oil to use for dressings. You can also use the peppers as part of a topping for *crostini* chopped up with anchovies and basil.

4 red peppers
Good olive oil to cover

3 sprigs of thyme
Zest of 2 lemons

Place the peppers on a roasting tray, drizzle with oil and roast in a hot oven until softened. Place in a plastic bag and seal the top. When the peppers have deflated and cooled, remove the seeds, peel and strain the juice into a kilner jar. Roughly tear the peppers and pack tightly in the jar along with the thyme and lemon zest. Cover with oil, seal and put them in the fridge. The oil may solidify in the fridge but don't worry, it will loosen when removed from the fridge after an hour or so.

Makes one Kilner jar

Mashed Potato

Mashed potatoes with fish can be so versatile. They can act as a carrier of extra flavour on the plate, leaving the fish to speak for itself. Try adding a handful of fresh herbs to the mash at the last minute or infusing the milk with saffron and enriching with cream, or finely slicing some spring onions into it at the last minute. They are also luxurious in a fish pie or smothered in fresh parsley sauce. This is how we make mashed potatoes at FishWorks. Use a good floury variety like King Edwards. The larger the potato the less you will have to peel but make sure you cut them into even chunks before boiling.

Boil the potatoes until tender, drain and then return to a low heat for a minute to ensure all the water has evaporated. Add some heated milk and a little butter cut into small chunks and get mashing. Work the potato until there are no lumps. Add a little more butter to your taste and a glug of double cream and then with a wire whisk work this in and season. It should be luxuriously creamy, not sloppy.

Flavours which work well – just add them in whatever quantity suits you:
chives, spring onions, dill, finely shredded watercress and rocket, bronze fennel, lemon juice and sea salt, tarragon, chervil, anchovy essence, olive oil instead of butter.

Flavours to infuse in the milk:
saffron, garlic, thyme, rosemary

See the Fishcakes recipe on page 168 to see what to do with leftovers.

FishWorks
Seafood Café
Cookbook

From the Grill

You can do almost anything with a hot grill and a grill plate. For the best results a barbecue outside the kitchen door will really give your food that wonderful summery taste. I keep one out there and regard it as part of my kitchen, but it's not a necessity. Using a grill plate is a really healthy way of cooking and it should remain on the cooker top all the time. I don't wash mine, I just give it a clean with a wire brush, and I never oil it. I always brush oil onto the fish as opposed to onto the grill, it keeps smokiness indoors to a minimum. A grill plate should always be hot before you use it. So give it five or ten minutes on the heat before the fish goes on. I have given simple recipes below because the grill is so quick and easy and the results are so impressive. Just choose one of them and an accompaniment that suits your mood and that's it.

These ten recipes show you how easy using a grill can be. Use any combination of herbs and oil from your store cupboard and make your own dishes. Be flexible and have some fun, it can be mastered in no time.

Remember, it is the fish that is the star and a good piece of it can need no more than a drizzle of good olive oil, lemon juice or just a sprinkling of sea salt. The grill is the ultimate tool for quick cooking with delicious results and I wouldn't be without mine.

Tuna with Rosemary and Sea Salt

Take a tuna steak, spike it with a few sprigs of rosemary, letting them hang out. Brush with oil and grill either side for 3 minutes. Drizzle with a bit of Salsa Verde (see page 34) and accompany it with Fennel, Mint, Coriander and Chilli Salad (see page 43).

Marlin with Fresh Thyme Leaf and Lemon

Marinate a marlin steak in lemon zest, garlic and thyme leaf for 15 minutes. Grill either side for 3 minutes, squeeze on some lemon juice and serve. Put a spoonful of salsa rossa (see page 34), on the side and accompany it with a bowl of Slow-roasted Tomatoes with Pesto (see page 44).

Charred Prawns with Indian Spices

Mix some curry paste with yoghurt and then add some chopped, fresh coriander. Split the prawns open down the back and marinate them in this mixture for an hour. Place on the grill plate for 6-7 minutes turning occasionally. Finish with a squeeze of lime.

Char-grilled Dover Sole with a Garlic Glaze

Ask your fishmonger to skin a Dover sole both sides. Brush it with oil and grill for 3 minutes on each side until the grill has marked it nicely. Finish it in a hot oven for a further 8-10 minutes. Lightly cover it with Hollandaise Sauce (see page 35) and pop it under the grill, not the grill plate, for 1-2 minutes until golden. Accompany with a green salad.

Grilled Sea Bass Fillet with Oregano, Lemon and Sea Salt

Take a fillet of sea bass, brush it with oil and sprinkle it with dried oregano. Grill it skin side down first for 3–4 minutes and then turn it over. Finish it with a squeeze of lemon and a sprinkle of crunchy sea salt. Perfect with a Greek salad.

Grilled Sardines with Garlic Butter

Brush a few sardines with oil and grill them either side for 3 minutes. Melt some garlic butter and pour over the top. Crusty bread and a lemon will do fine with this.

Grilled Salmon with Tarragon

Making sure the skin is scaled, take a small piece of salmon cut across the fillet. Brush it with oil and grill it skin side down for 4-5 minutes. Turn it over for a further 2-3 minutes. Warm up a spoonful of Béchamel Sauce (see page 36), add some cream and tarragon and pour over the top of your salmon. Accompany it with a bowl of creamy Mashed Potato (see page 47).

Grilled Swordfish with Garlic and Saffron

Brush a swordfish steak with oil and grill for 3 minutes each side. Melt some garlic butter, add a pinch of saffron and infuse for a few minutes. Spoon over the fish and finish with a squeeze of lemon.

Herb-smoked Lobster

This is definitely one for the outdoor grill. Split a cooked lobster in half and remove the meat from the tail. Spread some garlic butter in the shell, sprinkle on a selection of chopped herbs and lay the meat back in. Put the lobsters shell down on the grill and cover with an upside down casserole dish or similar. Place some bunches of rosemary and thyme on the charcoal and let the smoke go up inside the dish. The lobster will take on a wonderful herby fragrance.

Scallops with Sage and Bacon

Wrap 6 scallops individually with a sage leaf and then a thin rasher of bacon or pancetta. Place on a grill turning frequently for 4-5 minutes. Serve with a pot of Aioli (see page 37), and a green salad.

FishWorks
Seafood Café
Cookbook

The Recipes

The recipes that follow are my personal favourites. They are the practical realisation of my philosophy of cooking and eating fish. I hope that by reading the recipe titles and flicking through some of the recipes you will find that your taste buds come alive. I hope that you will suddenly feel the urge to race down to your local fishmonger and demand of him his finest, freshest fish, which you will then whisk home to create a great meal for astonished friends and family.

Many of the recipes appear regularly on FishWorks menus and are referred to as FishWorks Classics. A FishWorks logo appears on the top of the page of these classic recipes. Many of the other recipes here are ones that appear from time to time at our restaurants or regularly at my home when cooking for the family.

Deep-fried Fresh Anchovies

Fresh anchovies can be hard to find, but keep asking your fishmonger as they are occasionally available in this country. Just a handful, floured and shallow-fried, can be one of the most satisfying lunches there is. Just in case you were wondering, salted anchovies are merely fresh ones cured in salt to preserve them.

2 eggs, beaten

Handful of coriander, chopped

Splash of white wine

A few tbsp flour

A few tbsp polenta or fine breadcrumbs

5 or 6 anchovies per person, ask
    your fishmonger to fillet them for you

Oil for deep frying

Wedge of lemon

Pinch of sea salt

Mix together the egg, coriander and wine.

In another bowl mix together the flour and polenta or breadcrumbs.

Get your oil to 325°F/170°C, then dip each fillet in the egg then into the flour mixture and fry for 2 minutes until golden and crisp. Remove and drain on kitchen paper and serve with lemon, a pinch of sea salt, and lots of chilled rosé wine.

Serves 4

Marinated Anchovies with Mint and Chilli

These anchovies really are delicious and for those who always imagine anchovies to be cured in salt you are in for a surprise. They are produced in Italy by a small producer and are just cured in vinegar and olive oil. They are available in most good delicatessens now. They are silver in colour. This recipe is a good way of serving them for an instant starter or lunch. And it looks pretty on the plate too.

200g/7oz marinated anchovies
1 tbsp fresh mint leaves, chopped
1/2 small, mild chilli, finely diced

Juice of 1/2 lemon
4 handfuls of small salad leaves
Good olive oil for drizzling

Mix the first four ingredients together well and place in a small pile in the middle of each of your four plates. Dress the salad with a little olive oil and lemon juice and place a handful carefully on the top of the anchovies. Drizzle more good oil around the plate.

Serves 4

Anchovy and Broad Bean Crostini

This is a wonderful recipe for the summer. Perfect with a chilled glass of Prosecco in the mid-summer heat at a barbecue or to kick off a lazy Sunday lunch in the garden. Good as a light lunch as well – just make them bigger.

8 slices of ciabata
Drizzle of good olive oil
Sprinkling of sea salt
1 clove of garlic
100g/4oz fresh broad beans, blanched and

the skin removed
Handful of mint, chopped
Juice of ½ lemon
8 salted anchovy fillets

Slice the bread across the loaf, brush with olive oil and sprinkle with milled sea salt and grill on a hot grill plate until just charred. Set aside ready for topping.

Place the garlic and half of the broad beans into the bowl of your hand processor and blitz until smooth. Transfer to a bowl and add the remaining broad beans – this can be done in advance and kept in the fridge until needed. Just before serving add the fresh mint and a squeeze of lemon juice. Spread a tablespoon on top of each toasted ciabata, add two chopped salted anchovy fillets and drizzle with olive oil.

Serves 4

Try this too...

Substitute the broad beans for chopped tomatoes, olive oil, fresh basil, garlic and lemon juice, spoon on top of the bread and top with anchovies.

Grilled Sea Bass
with Toasted Walnuts and Basil Leaf

Sea bass doesn't really need anything doing to it; its flavour is fine and a drizzle of good olive oil and a squeeze of lemon is enough to complement. This dressing is based on the classic pesto but using walnuts instead. It works.

1/4 pint good olive oil

4 thick fillets of sea bass weighing 150g each,
  (try to get them from a big fish)

Handful shelled walnut halves

2 handfuls of basil leaves

1 clove of garlic, pasted

Tbsp grated Parmesan

Tsp capers

Squeeze lemon juice

Pinch sea salt

Oil the fish on the skin side and start on a hot grill plate and then carefully remove and finish in a hot oven for 4-5 minutes. To make the sauce toast the walnuts in a dry pan and then roughly blend the remaining ingredients and then serve a spoonful with the fish.

Serves 4

Sea Bass Roasted with Rosemary, Lemon and Sea Salt

The sea bass is one of the most highly prized fish of the sea. Absolute freshness here is all important. It is a fish that is so easy to cook, as it really needs nothing doing to it. This method of roasting it with rosemary is my favourite. For a dinner party it looks grand just presented as a whole fish dressed with a fragrant olive oil with all the rosemary branches burnt from the heat of the cooker and a wonderful crisp silver skin. Your guests can help themselves first by taking the flesh from the top of the fillet exposing the bone, and then removing it to make the bottom fillet accessible. To accompany, fresh spinach with cream and garlic is ideal.

Sea bass – 2 fish weighing 450g/1lb each, scaled and gutted	Lemon
	Sea salt
Fresh rosemary	Olive oil

Slash the sea bass twice on each side diagonally to the bone. Into the slashes and belly cavity put the fresh rosemary – let it all hang out, as it will burn giving an extra flavour to the dish. Put on a roasting tray and rub the fish with olive oil (not your best one) and then sprinkle with sea salt and put into a pre-heated oven at 400°F/200°C/gas mark 6 and roast uncovered for 15-18 minutes. The flesh should be white, the skin crisp and easily taken off the bone. It can be started on the grill pan and finished in the oven if you like a more grilled flavour.

Serve whole, drizzled with a squeeze of lemon and good olive oil.

Serves 2

Baked Sea Bream with Sweet and Sour Onions

Although the bream is baked in the oven *en papillote* (see page 156) the fish is actually steamed inside, which keeps it wonderfully juicy. The steam is flavoured with ginger and garlic which infuses the fish. The sweet and sour onions that accompany are just perfection. You can make a large batch and keep them in the fridge in a sealed jar. They work as an accompaniment to any fish or can be shredded into a noodle salad.

2 sea bream weighing 450g/1lb each, scaled
    and filleted
25mm/1" of root ginger, peeled and sliced
1 clove of garlic, sliced
Sea salt
3-4 tbsp water
175g/6oz butter
2 onions, finely sliced
275ml/8 floz white wine vinegar
2 tbsp of balsamic vinegar

1 carrot, chopped
1 stick of celery, chopped
1 shallot, finely sliced
2 heads of dried star anise
2 cloves
6 white peppercorns
2 dried bay leaves
175g/6oz caster sugar
Glass of white wine
Handful of coriander, chopped

First prepare the bream fillets for the oven. Place the ginger and garlic onto the centre of a square of foil or paper and put the fish on the top. Season with salt and fold up the sides to make a tight seal around the fish and add 3-4 tablespoons of water. Place on a baking tray ready for the oven.

Melt the butter and add the onions, then over a very low heat cook until softened and starting to caramelise. Remove from the heat and set aside.

Put the remaining ingredients into a pan, except the coriander. Bring to the boil and simmer for 6–7 minutes, remove from the heat and allow the flavours to infuse; an hour is sufficient.

Drain off the vegetables. Cook the bream in a pre-heated oven for 7-8 minutes. Remove from the parcel and put on a plate. Add a few tablespoons of the sweet and sour mixture to the onions and gently warm through. Add the coriander and put a spoonful on top of the bream.

Serves 4 as a starter

Stuffed Clams

I like to use Palourde or soft shell clams for this dish as I find them meatier and more juicy. Delicious with this simple garlic breadcrumb topping. A plate of these is a fantastic prelude to any barbecue or served just as they are with a glass of wine for an informal lunch.

Allow 450g/1lb of clams per person
Small splash of white wine
100g/4oz unsalted butter
2 cloves of garlic, pasted

1 tbsp of fresh, chopped tarragon
 (or parsley if you prefer)
Handful of fresh breadcrumbs
Pinch of sea salt

Place the clams and the wine into a large saucepan with a tight fitting lid and steam open. When they have cooled, remove the empty shell from the clams and place the bottom shell containing the clam meat side by side on a serving dish. Add the butter, the garlic and the tarragon to the remaining juices in the pan and allow the flavours to infuse for 2-3 minutes, then add the breadcrumbs until all the juices have been soaked up. Place a teaspoon on the top of each clam. Finish under a hot grill until crisp and serve with a squeeze of lemon juice.

Serves 1

Try this too...

If you can't get clams use mussels instead and for a bit more of a luxurious finish spoon a little Hollandaise Sauce (see page 35) over the top and glaze under a grill for 1-2 minutes.

Spaghetti with Clams, Chilli, Parsley and Olive Oil

Try to buy large fat, juicy Palourde clams for this dish. The better the clam, the better the sauce. All you want to taste is fresh, sweet, salty clam juice, fragrant parsley and a touch of heat from the chilli. It's quick, delicious and easy.

1 garlic clove, pasted
1 small, mild chilli, finely chopped
Olive oil
Small squeeze of lemon juice

300g/11oz clams
150g/5oz spaghetti, pre-cooked and rinsed
Handful of parsley, chopped

Gently sweat the garlic and chilli in the olive oil. Add a dash of lime, boil for a minute, and then add the clams allowing them to steam open. This will take 3-4 minutes. Be sure to discard any which do not open. Add the pasta and allow it to warm through, then finish with a handful of parsley and serve. I often cook this in my favourite copper pan and serve from it at the table, letting the whole family dig in.

Serves 1

Cockles with Smoked Bacon

Fresh cockles in the shell taste of nothing else but the sea, and the best ones I have found come from the Gower in Wales, and in particular Pencloud where the cockles are still harvested at low tide by families who have been doing so almost since the beginning of recorded time. Not only does this recipe call for good fresh cockles but also the addition of good smoked bacon.

A splash of dry white wine (and I mean just a splash!)

1 clove of garlic, crushed

50g/2oz smoked bacon

450g/1lb cockles (as a main) or 250g/9oz cockles (as a starter)

50ml/2fl oz double cream

Handful of parsley, chopped

Take a good sized saucepan, large enough to hold the cockles, with a tight fitting lid. Add a splash of wine, the garlic and smoked bacon, then add the cockles. Replace the lid and allow the liquor to heat and the cockles to steam open. Gently shake the pan at regular intervals, the cockles are cooked when the shells have opened. If any do not open discard them. Spoon the cockles and smoked bacon mix into large bowls, add some cream to the remaining liquor, add the chopped parsley and pour over. Easy!

Serves 1

Braised Cod Steak
with Muscadet and Rosemary

I prefer cod steaks to fillets. I like the look of them on the plate and I like the way the flesh just flakes away from the bone. The best steaks are those taken from the fish just behind the gut cavity. When you cut through the fish here, the steaks remain round. Rosemary is a fragrant herb and is rarely associated with delicate fish like cod but I think its perfume really flavours the sauce well and somehow brings the whole dish together. This recipe works equally well with fish such as whiting, some firm gurnard fillets from a large fish, or one of my favourites, hake.

Knob of butter
1 leek, finely shredded
4 sprigs of rosemary
1 clove of garlic, pasted
150ml/5fl oz of Muscadet

150ml/5fl oz of double cream
4 cod steaks weighing 175g/6oz each
Pinch of sea salt
Turn of black pepper

Melt half the butter in a heavy based frying pan. Add the leek, rosemary and garlic and cook until soft. Add the Muscadet. Turn the heat up and boil off the alcohol. This will take about 1-2 minutes. Add the cream, bring back to the boil and pour this mixture into the bottom of a ceramic roasting tray.

Wipe out the frying pan, heat some vegetable oil and sear the cod steaks until golden on either side. This will take about 2-3 minutes. Then place the cod steaks on top of the cream and leek mixture, cover with foil and place in a medium oven for around 10 minutes.

To serve, lift each steak out with a fish slice, retaining some vegetables under each one and drizzle the rest of the sauce around the plate.

Serves 4

Cornish Cod with Cockles and Tarragon

There is so much flavour in shellfish that you can usually rely on their juices to help give you a wonderful sauce. In this dish, the sea water from the cockles is mixed with fresh, aniseedy tarragon, a touch of cream and chopped tomato which makes a wonderfully easy sauce to accompany fresh roasted fillet of cod. I would recommend this as a quick supper or, because of its colour and texture, in a bowl sprinkled with cockle shells as a dinner party dish. When buying the cod fillet ask your fishmonger for the loin which is the thick part of the fillet.

150g/5oz prime cod fillet per person
Splash of white wine
1 clove of garlic, crushed
200g/7oz of fresh cockles

50ml/2fl oz double cream
1 tomato, insides removed and the flesh
    chopped into fine dice
Handful of fresh tarragon

Add some vegetable oil to a non-stick pan, lightly season the cod and cook for 2-3 minutes, turning the fillets once. Transfer to a very hot oven and cook until nearly 'set'. Just before the cod is ready to be removed from the oven add the wine to a pan with a tight fitting lid along with the garlic and the cockles and allow to steam gently for 2-3 minutes.

When the cockles have opened (and you have discarded any that haven't) remove half of the shells and leave the remainder in the sauce for decoration on the plate. Add the cream, tomato and lots of fresh tarragon and bring gently to the boil. To assemble the dish, place the cod in the middle of a deep bowl and liberally spoon the sauce over and around the cod.

Serves 1

Try this too...

Use this sauce with any of the following fish – turbot fillet, lemon sole fillet, haddock fillet, gurnard fillet, weaver fish fillet, or add a few mussels, clams or winkles to the sauce and make it a mixed shellfish sauce with tarragon. Ah, the versatility of fish!

Deep-fried Salt Cod with Aioli

This dish is a great way of using salt cod. Everyone loves it. I think it is the fried thing and the garlic. They are just like little fishcakes and irresistible as a nibble.

400g/14oz salt cod (see page 72)
2 tbsp flour
2 eggs, beaten
50g/2oz fresh breadcrumbs

Oil for deep frying
Lemon wedges for serving
As much aioli as you like for dipping
  (see page 37)

Chill the brandade. When chilled make into little balls the size of walnuts. Roll in flour, then beaten egg and finally in breadcrumbs.

Heat your oil to 190C/350°F and deep fry for 2-3 minutes until crisp and golden. Drain on some kitchen paper and serve with a lemon wedge and a bowl of aioli.

Serves 4

Brandade with Poached Egg and Olive Sauce

Brandade is a dish made from fresh salted cod fillet with loads of garlic. In my recipe I have added fresh parsley which gives it a lovely fresh edge. You can buy cod ready-salted, however, I prefer the flavour of home-salted cod and for this recipe this is what I have used. If you do buy cod that is ready salted you will need to make the soaking time twice as long. In many parts of Italy, France and Portugal you will find large barrels filled with cod ready-soaked for use in the kitchen.

The brandade in this recipe can be served either simply as an appetiser or more luxuriously with a runny poached egg. If you can get large, fresh duck eggs this will add even more of a richness to the dish. If you don't feel brave enough to serve this as a starter or for a lunch then try making a small amount and giving your guests some lightly toasted bread for dunking and a bowl of black olives to make a wondrous appetiser.

To make the brandade

250ml/8fl oz milk
250g/9oz prime cod fillet (you could use
   whiting, haddock or other white fish)
1 clove of garlic

600ml/1 pint good olive oil
Handful of parsley, chopped
Squeeze of lemon juice
1 bay leaf

To make the olive sauce

1 tbsp crushed coriander seeds
4 tbsp good quality, fruity olive oil
1 tomato, sliced and finely diced

Handful of fresh green or purple basil, shredded
Juice of 1/2 a lemon
10 pitted black olives, finely chopped

4 poached duck eggs

Salting cod
Take a plastic container and lay an inch of coarse rock salt across the bottom, lay the fish on top and completely bury in rock salt and leave in the fridge for 24 hours. The salt will extract much of the moisture from the fish, leaving it quite stiff. Before use you must soak the cod in cold water for 1-2 hours, changing the water at least 3 times which will remove much of the saltiness.

To make the brandade
Gently warm the milk and place the soaked fish into it. Leave this to poach over a low heat for 5-6 minutes. Take out the cod and when cool enough to handle remove any skin or bones so you are left with just flesh. In your food processor blitz the clove of garlic to a fine paste then add the fish and blitz further for 2-3 minutes. Then gently, as with mayonnaise, pour a stream of good olive oil into the mixture until it starts to emulsify and thicken. Finish with a handful of chopped parsley and a squeeze of lemon juice. It should taste lightly salty, fresh and with a wonderful overtone of fresh garlic. If green garlic is in season, which will be round about April or May time, then this is the best garlic to use. You can serve the brandade at room

temperature or gently warm it in a pan with a further glug of olive oil.

To make the olive sauce
Add the crushed coriander seeds to the olive oil and place on a warm stove. You must keep the temperature at a level so low that you could put your finger in without feeling discomfort. Remove from the heat and add the tomato, fresh basil leaf, a squeeze of lemon juice and a tiny sprinkling of milled sea salt. Finally add the black olives. This makes a wonderful, colourful sauce which looks absolutely stunning on a white plate.

To assemble the dish
Warm the brandade and place a few tablespoons in the middle of each plate. Top with a poached egg and spoon the black olive sauce around the plate and over the top of the egg.

Serves 4

Fresh Spaghetti with Crab, Chilli and Parsley

This is a really simple dish, great for lunch or a starter before dinner but better served 'family style', in a big bowl in the middle of the table with everyone helping themselves.

400g/14oz spaghetti
1 tbsp good olive oil
1 clove of garlic, chopped
1 shallot, finely chopped
1 red chilli, finely chopped

150g/5oz fresh brown crab meat
Juice of ½ lemon
50g/2oz fresh white crab meat
Handful of flat leaf parsley, chopped
Salt and pepper to season

Bring a large pan of salted water to the boil and cook the spaghetti until *al dente*.

In a separate pan add the olive oil and gently sweat the shallot and garlic. Add the chilli. On a gentle heat, stir in the crab meat and warm through. Add a squeeze of lemon juice and the parsley, season to taste and then toss with the cooked spaghetti.

Serves 4

Crab Omelette Thermidor

This is an indulgent supper for one or two. There is something luxurious about this dish – I think it is because it seems to sum up comfort food.

4 eggs
150ml/¼ pint Béchamel sauce (as used in the Lobster Thermidor recipe on page 92)

50g/2oz fresh picked white crab meat and 25g/1oz brown meat,
1 tbsp fresh tarragon leaves, chopped
25g/1oz of butter

Whisk the eggs and set aside. Warm the Béchamel sauce and add the crabmeat and tarragon.

In a frying pan, melt the butter and when hot pour in half the egg to make the first omelette. With a spoon scrape from the edge of the pan to the middle to allow the uncooked egg to come into contact with the pan. Just before it sets add half the Béchamel and crab mixture and then fold the omelette over and serve immediately. Repeat for the second omelette.

Serves 3

Cornish Crab Salad with Gazpacho Sauce

Summer is the time of year when native brown crabs are plentiful. You can buy ready picked crab meat but often it is pasteurised and I think loses some of its flavour. And anyway there is nothing like wrestling with the beast yourself and carefully picking out every last juicy piece of delicious meat. The sauce here, based on the classic Spanish gazpacho, sets the whole dish off perfectly.

1/4 red pepper, finely diced
1/4 green pepper, finely diced
1/4 medium cucumber, finely diced
1 pint of tomato juice
1 shallot, finely diced
Splash of red wine vinegar
Pinch of sea salt

1 cock crab, about 1kg/2 1/4 lb, cooked
  (brown and white meat)
Salad leaves, about 4 handfuls
  (rocket and watercress work well)
Lemon juice and olive oil
  (for dressing the salad leaves)

For the sauce, mix together the peppers, cucumber, tomato juice, shallot and vinegar and season to taste.

To serve, spoon some brown crabmeat onto the centre of each plate and then spoon some white meat on top. Garnish this with a small handful of dressed salad leaves and then drizzle your sauce around the edge of the crab. Serve with a crisp Muscadet and fresh brown bread.

Serves 4

Baked Crab
with a Garlic and Parsley Crumb

I was never a fan of hot crab dishes. I suppose nothing had ever surpassed the flavour of a freshly boiled and cooled crab eaten with fresh mayonnaise. And then I visited Singapore where I fell for Singapore Chilli Crab and Black Pepper Crab. They have a different species of crab there called the mud crab, which has a denser flesh than our native crabs. I tried, without success, to recreate the dishes I enjoyed in Singapore. But in trying I stumbled on this dish. Nothing Far Eastern about it, but great all the same. By 'dressed crabs' I mean all the meat removed and put back into the top shell. Your fishmonger will be able to do this for you or occasionally you can buy them ready prepared and unpasteurised.

5 cloves of garlic

50g/2oz of melted butter

½ an onion, finely chopped

Good handful of fresh flat leaf parsley, chopped

4 small dressed crabs

1 tbsp of bronze fennel, finely chopped

Breadcrumbs

150ml/5fl oz Hollandaise sauce (see page 35)

First paste up the garlic and place a teaspoon into the butter, which you have melted along with a good pinch of parsley.

In a heavy-based pan gently fry the onion and the remaining garlic till softened. Mix in the crab meat. Just warm it through and do not cook for too long. Finally, add the fennel and the remaining parsley and spoon the mixture back into the shells.

Mix the breadcrumbs with the melted butter and parsley and pack tightly over the top of the crab mixture. Top each shell with a spoonful or two of Hollandaise sauce and place under the grill until golden. Serve on a bed of rock salt, which will stabilise the crab shell while your guest's gasp with admiration as they tuck in.

Serves 4

Crab Chowder

This is based on our popular FishWorks Clam Chowder. A light broth, enriched with fresh crabmeat and finished with cream and parsley. It's another ten minute dish which is great if you have to knock up a quick lunch for six people or more. You could always just make it for one with leftover crabmeat instead of resorting to the perennial crab cake!

Olive oil
2 sticks of celery, finely chopped
1 fennel bulb, tops and fronds
1 onion, finely chopped
3 cloves of garlic, chopped
1 small, mild chilli, finely chopped
3 carrots, peeled and finely chopped
Splash of Pernod

White and dark meat from 1 medium-sized
  cock crab
1.2l/2 pints good fish stock
600ml/1 pint double cream
2 tomatoes peeled, deseeded and chopped
Handful of fresh flat leaf parsley, chopped
Salt and pepper

Gently fry in olive oil the celery, fennel, onion, garlic, chilli and carrots until softened. Add the Pernod and boil off the alcohol for a minute. Add the brown crab meat and stir well with the vegetables. Pour in the fish stock, bring to a gentle boil and then finish by stirring in the cream, white crab meat, tomatoes and parsley. Check seasoning and serve to a round of well deserved applause.

Serves 4

Boiled Crayfish with Dill

Crayfish are fresh-water creatures which resemble lobsters. Don't confuse them with crawfish which are in fact spiny or rock lobsters occasionally caught off our coast (unfortunately not in great numbers), more often found on barbecues in the Caribbean or the Far East. You may find crayfish hard to come by, however, ask your fishmonger who will more often than not know a local who fishes for them. They are considered pests by many, so when they are being fished it is usually in great quantity from a river or lake. This makes them reasonable in price so it is worth buying a bucketful and getting your friends around for a delicious and entertaining experience.

1 onion, chopped
1 bulb of garlic, cut in half
Glass of brandy

2 big bunches of fresh dill, roughly chopped
2kg/4½lb live crayfish
Sea salt

In a large pan gently sweat the onions until softened but do not brown. If the oil gets too hot add a little water and continue to cook. Add the two halves of the garlic bulb and then the brandy. Boil for a minute to burn off the alcohol. Add enough water to ensure that the crayfish, when added, will be covered and the roughly chopped dill. Make sure you add the stalks as well, as they are packed with flavour. Bring to the boil, and add the crayfish and a tablespoon of salt. Bring back to the boil and gently cook for 8 minutes. The crayfish will change colour dramatically to a deep red.

Place in a large bowl with the juices and plonk on the table for everyone to get stuck in. Equip them with bibs and napkins and a handful of picks and crackers. Show the uninitiated how to eat them by doing the following:

Remove the body from the head with a quick twist
Remove the shell from the tail
Suck out the juices from the head (be brave)
Use your picks, crackers, teeth and fingers to get the meat from the claws and anywhere else you see a bit lurking
Have fun!

Serves 4

Moroccan-style Gurnard with Clams

Gurnard is a fish which is talked about a great deal these days and that's as it should be. Its cheap, delicious and most importantly is in plentiful supply. I first saw it in Bere Regis, Dorset, when I was about four or five: my grandmother was negotiating with a surprised fisherman to buy his catch. I can still remember this bright red colourful fish that looked so alien to anything I had ever seen before. She managed to stretch it to feed all of us for supper that evening. Its flesh is firm and tasty and stands up to slow braising. In this recipe it is cooked with a spice mix called chermoula, typical of North African cuisine. To make this dish really authentic you need to use preserved lemons; you can buy them in some supermarkets but they are so easy to make and will keep for up to 8 weeks, that I insist you make them at home. The juice that develops is also good for dressings. Although this dish is heavily flavoured it doesn't mean that the flavour of gurnard needs to be disguised. A good thick fillet simply grilled or barbecued makes for a perfect meal. Gurnard comes in three different species: tub gurnard which are larger, grey gurnard which are striped, and my favourite, red.

8 tbsp olive oil
6 cloves of garlic, pasted
1 onion, finely chopped
2 tsp ground cumin
1 green pepper, finely sliced
1 tsp ground turmeric
Good handful of coriander, chopped

Good handful of parsley, chopped
12 large black olives
1 preserved lemon, roughly chopped
Pinch of salt
4 fillets of gurnard, skinned – they should
    weigh about 175g/6oz each
Good handful of clams

Mix together all the ingredients except the fish. Place half the mixture in a casserole dish with a heavy lid and put the fish on top. Put the remaining marinade on top of the fish and marinate in the fridge overnight.

Before cooking pour over a cup of water and add the clams. Bake in a hot oven for 15 minutes and serve with couscous.

Serves 4

Hake with Clams and Bacon

This dish is cooked in a bag in the oven and is simplicity itself. All the moisture and delicate flavours of the fish are retained beautifully. The clams add their delicate sea-like juices to the finished sauce and with a squeeze of lemon and the flavour of light smoked bacon it makes a great dish suitable for a family meal or a supper party.

4 hake cutlets, about 225g/8oz per person
100g/4oz smoked bacon, chopped
Handful of clams, mussels or cockles
Dash of white wine

Handful of parsley, torn
1 leek, finely sliced
Squeeze of lemon juice
Dash of cream

Place the fish onto four squares of tin foil or inside a roasting bag. Sprinkle over the smoked bacon. Place the shellfish around the hake (the main ingredients are the clams but you could add raw langoustines or prawns as well to make a light stew). Fold up the sides of the foil and add a good slug of white wine. Throw in the torn parsley and then seal up the foil into a parcel or seal the roasting bag. Place on a baking or roasting tray and bake for 8-10 minutes on 400°F/200°C/gas mark 6.

Gently sweat the leeks in butter for 5-6 minutes and finish with a dash of cream.

To serve, remove from the bag and serve the fish placed on top of the leeks with the opened clams, cockles or mussels placed around the fish. Lastly, before taking the dish to the table, add a squeeze of lemon juice.

Serves 4

Crisp-fried Herring Roes with Sauce Gribiche

This is definitely a fond childhood memory. Mum used to cook these for me on toast. They were a real treat, as indeed they are now as you don't come across them that often. They can be bought frozen but I like buying fresh, fat herring, curing the fillets and eating the roes fresh the same night. There are two types of roe in the herring, 'hard' from the female and 'soft' from the male – I prefer the soft but the choice is yours. I always select my herring by turning the fish over and squeezing its stomach – you can see the roe appearing from the hole just behind the bottom fin, the soft ones will appear white and milky and the hard ones more coarse and slightly darker. Sauce gribiche is a piquant egg-based sauce which I have often eaten served with sweetbreads. I don't know why but the two seem similar to me, so I tried it out with the roes one day and found it delicious. For me, herring roes are like the *foie gras* of the sea, only cheaper.

For the sauce gribiche

250ml/8fl oz milk	Handful of parsley, chopped
1 clove of garlic	Squeeze of lemon juice
600ml/1 pint good olive oil	1 bay leaf
150g/5oz herring roes	1 egg, beaten
2 tbsp flour	Handful of fresh breadcrumbs

First make the sauce by separating the yolks and whites. Put the yolks in a bowl and mash together with the mustard and vinegar. Continue to stir whilst adding a steady stream of olive oil until a smooth paste consistency is reached. Stir in the capers and tarragon. Then finely grate the whites of the egg and stir those in. Finish with a squeeze of lemon. From here on the cooking is easy.

Preheat your fryer to 325°F/170°C. Dip the roes in flour, then the beaten egg, then the breadcrumbs and fry for 2-3 minutes until crisp and golden. Divide equally onto the plates and spoon some sauce next to the roes with maybe a small rocket salad to garnish.

Serves 2

Try this too...

Lightly flour the roes and gently fry in a little oil and butter until light golden in colour and serve on toast or, as Elizabeth David suggests, bake them in a dish with a little wine topped with breadcrumbs. Either way they must be tried, as you will be missing something if you don't.

Pan-roasted John Dory
with a Thyme and Wild Mushroom Risotto

Risotto and fish are a great combination. John Dory is perfect to eat with risotto but turbot or brill would work just as well.

1.2l/2 pints fish or chicken stock
75g/3oz dried Porcini mushrooms
1 shallot, chopped
1 clove of garlic, chopped
1 cup of Carnaroli or Arborio rice
3 sprigs of thyme

50g/2oz fresh wild mushrooms or field
   mushrooms, chopped
25g/1oz Parmesan
25g/1oz unsalted butter
Sea salt
4 x 150g/5oz John Dory fillets

First start the risotto by warming the fish stock and setting aside to keep warm.

In a separate bowl soak the dried mushrooms in 150ml/5fl oz of warm water for 30 minutes. Remove the mushrooms and chop, keeping the soaking liquid.

In a saucepan gently heat the shallots and garlic in a little olive oil. Add the rice and gently fry for 2-3 minutes until translucent and coated in oil. Add the thyme and then the retained mushroom juice. Keep covering the rice with ladles of the warmed fish stock until the rice absorbs it, stirring all the time. When the rice is *al dente*, or just firm, add the dried and fresh mushrooms and whisk in the Parmesan and the butter. The risotto should be wonderfully creamy. Check seasoning.

To cook the fish, heat some oil in a pan and get it really hot, then fry the fish until golden on both sides. Place in a hot oven and finish cooking for 4-5 minutes. To serve, place some risotto in a bowl and lay the fish on top.

Serves 4

Pan-roasted John Dory with Chive Mash, Green Beans and Lemon Butter

John Dory has to be considered a luxury. It's a wonderful fish to eat but sadly in proportion to its size it does not yield an awful lot of flesh and therefore can seem expensive. Once tried, however, the expense will seem irrelevant. This makes for a hearty supper. Green beans are one of my favourites surpassed only by the first of the season's runner beans. Good mashed potato is worth labouring over and I love flavoured mash – here I have just added handfuls of freshly chopped chives which add a lovely crunch and flavour to the potato.

4 John Dory fillets weighing 150g/5oz each
   (a large fillet from larger fish cut down into this
   size will give you a much better experience)
100g/4oz green beans
Good handful of fresh chives, finely chopped

400g/14oz mashed potato (see page 47)
75g/3oz butter
Handful of fresh parsley, chopped
Juice of 1 lemon
Pinch of sea salt

Heat some vegetable oil in a frying pan until smoking and lay the John Dory fillets into the pan. Fry for 3-4 minutes until crisp and golden. Finish the cooking in a hot oven for a further 4-5 minutes.

While the fish finishes cooking, blanch the beans in boiling salted water, drain and set aside. Mix the chives into the cooked mashed potato. Make the lemon butter as in the grilled sole recipe with lemon and parsley butter (see page 136).

To serve, place a spoonful of mashed potato on a plate, the beans alongside it and a John Dory fillet on top of the two vegetables. Then spoon the lemon and parsley butter over the fish and around the plate. This dish could also be topped with a small handful of fresh salad shoots dressed in nothing but lemon juice and olive oil.

Serves 4

Try this too...

If you want to change the flavour of the mash, try adding tarragon and some chopped shallots, or replace the herb in the butter with basil, marjoram or bronze fennel.

Kippers

The only things you need to accompany kippers are the Sunday papers and a freshly brewed pot of tea. They are simple to cook, a challenge to eat, but worth every second of fiddling through the herring's fine bones. Try and avoid kippers which are chemically smoked and contain dye. They are easy to spot as they are a deep orange. Try to buy plump herrings which have been split and opened up and retain a light to deep brown colour. Some specialist smokeries, like the Alchiltibuie Brewery Smoke House in Scotland produce marvellous kippers which are available by mail order at FishWorks. Robert Wing in Cornwall buys only the finest herrings for our restaurants and smokes them perfectly with a traditional cure over oak chippings. These too are available by mail order (see page 23 for details of Robert Wing).

I like my kippers just simply grilled, brushed with butter, and sometimes eaten with a small pot of marmalade. If you don't fancy grilling kippers, then just take a jug of hot water and immerse the kipper into it, head down with the tail sticking out of the top. Leave it for 6-7 minutes and then serve. They can also be cooked *en papillote* (see page 156 for method) with a little butter and a teaspoon of whisky or during the summer they can just be laid on to a barbecue, gently warmed over the wood fire and either eaten as they are or peeled from the bones and tossed into a Caesar or green salad.

When a kipper is traditionally produced, it is split from the top of the back through to the bottom of the fish and it can be opened up with the bone on one side and just the rib cage on the other. It amazes me that most restaurants and hotels in which I've eaten kippers serve them to you with the bones facing up. I have found that the simplest way is to turn the kipper over until you're faced with the flesh. You can then eat from the top of the bones saving you the job of navigating your way through them.

Grilled Kippers with a Citrus Sauce

A great leisurely breakfast. One for the garden on a hot mid-summer's morning.

4 whole kippers   125g/4oz butter
Zest of 1 orange   Juice of 1 lemon
Zest of 1 lemon   Fresh parsley, chopped

Gently cook the kippers under a pre-heated grill for 4-5 minutes.

Put the orange and lemon zest in a pan with the butter and heat until the mixture is bubbling gently. Stir in the lemon juice and parsley. Place the kippers on serving plates, pour the sauce over the fish and serve with crusty bread to mop up the sauce or perhaps a heap of buttery mashed potato.

Serves 4

Langoustines with Fennel Mayonnaise

Fresh langoustines are luxurious. I don't think fish gets any better. The flesh is firm and wonderfully sweet and worth the effort of breaking into the shell. A pile of these, freshly boiled and cooled and some lovely, well-made mayonnaise flavoured with fennel or garlic, surpasses almost anything. They will often be hard to find and can be expensive. Always try to buy live langoustines, the quality is far superior to those that have either been preserved by a dipping process or frozen.

As many live langoustines as you feel you can eat
2 egg yolks
1 tsp Dijon mustard
150ml/¼ pint vegetable oil
150ml/¼ pint olive oil

1 tbsp tarragon, finely chopped
Handful of fresh bronze fennel, chopped
Pinch of salt
Juice of 1 lemon

Put the egg yolks in a bowl with the Dijon mustard and whisk. Gently, in a thin stream, pour in the vegetable and olive oils which have been mixed together. Keep whisking until an emulsion is formed. When all the oil has been added you should end up with a thick, creamy mayonnaise. Add the herb, the salt and the lemon and leave in the fridge for an hour to chill and for the flavours to develop.

Bring a large pan of salted water to a rolling boil, then add the langoustines and cook for 6-7 minutes. Remove from the pan and immerse in a single bowl of cold water to stop the cooking process. When cooled, serve a pile of langoustines with a small pot of the mayonnaise and some crisp lettuce leaves dressed in lemon juice, sea salt and olive oil.

To get the best out of eating a langoustine
Twist the body from the head and then suck out the juices and meat from inside the head. Go on, you've probably not done it before, but just close your eyes and you will savour the richness of the dark meat and the fresh taste of the sea. Before you attack the body, if the langoustines are big enough, break open the claws, either with some crackers, your fingers or, carefully, with your teeth (sorry dentists!). While the meat inside the claw is minimal, the flavour rewards the effort. Finally, you are ready for the body which will contain the greatest pleasure of all. Turn the langoustine over with its back facing away from you and break the shell away from the side with your thumbs and forefingers until you have peeled all the shell from the meat leaving it whole and inviting. Finally, one good dunk into the mayonnaise, close your eyes again, and then chew.

Fried Langoustines

This dish really could be part of a *Fritto Misto* (see page 153) but I often sit down to a plate of fresh langoustines which have been lightly coated in flour and fried. They are wonderfully sticky on the outside of the shell which you suck off while peeling and eating them. You can also use fresh prawns, chunks of lobster or small crabs for this dish.

Olive oil for frying

1 clove of garlic, bashed

16 medium-to-large-sized live langoustines

Flour for coating

A little butter

Handful of fresh flat parsley leaves, chopped

Juice of ½ lemon

Sea salt

Heat the olive oil in a frying pan and add the garlic clove. Spike it with a fork and swirl it round in the oil so that the oil takes on the flavour of the garlic. Dust the langoustines lightly in flour and add to the oil. Move them around and fry gently for 7-8 minutes.

Place onto a serving dish. Add a little butter to the olive oil, a handful of parsley and lemon juice and pour over the langoustines. You need nothing else to accompany this apart from a finger bowl and hard-crusted, freshly baked bread, although a little plate of Anchovy and Broad Bean Crostini (see page 60) works well as finger food to accompany.

Serves 4

Spaghetti with Fresh Lobster, Basil and Pine Nuts

This is a lovely way of bulking out fresh, sweet lobster meat with a delicious mix of light Mediterranean-style flavours.

Clove of garlic, pasted
Few tbsp good quality olive oil
1 tbsp pine nuts
Freshly cooked lobster, with the meat removed
  from the tail, head and claw
100g/4oz dried spaghetti

2 tbsp fresh pesto (see page 36)
Sea salt
Handful of fresh basil leaves – purple or
  green – torn
Juice of 1 lemon

Over a very gentle heat warm the garlic in the olive oil, stirring all the while to make sure the olive oil is well flavoured with the garlic. The oil must become intensely flavoured. Add the pine nuts and the lobster meat on a gentle heat as too fierce a heat will toughen the ready-cooked lobster meat.

In a separate pan cook the spaghetti in boiling salted water and drain, then add to the lobster and olive oil, and stir in the pesto. Finally, add the basil leaves, stir well and finish with a sprinkle of sea salt and a squeeze of lemon juice. To serve, place the lobster shell on a plate and fill it with the spaghetti, allowing it to spill over the bottom of the tail.

Serves 2

Try this too...

This recipe works with small cock crabs or crayfish, cooked in the same way and served in the shell and with a dill pesto rather than basil, or langoustines with a chilli and fennel pesto and clams.

The Seafood Café Lobster Thermidor

For me I think this is as good a way to cook lobster as there is. it sums up luxury and is a great way of doing a lobster justice. This recipe is based on a classic with a few extra touches. It is simple and delicious and will be the star of any dinner party.

4 live lobsters, about 750g/1lb 10oz each	1 tbsp flour
1 onion	1 tsp English mustard
1 bay leaf	2 cloves of garlic, crushed
8 black peppercorns, whole	1 shot of brandy
200ml/¹/₃ pint milk	Handful of fresh tarragon leaves, chopped
25g/1oz unsalted butter	Sea salt and pepper

First of all bring a large pan of salted water to the boil and add the live lobsters. Cook for 8-10 minutes. Remove from the water and allow to cool and then cut in half lengthways from the head to the tail. Remove all the meat, separating the dark meat and the coral (present in females) from the white meat and pick all the meat from the claws. Reserve the shells as these will be used for serving.

Make the sauce base by placing the onion, bay leaf, peppercorns and milk into a pan and bringing to the boil. Simmer for 2-3 minutes and remove from the heat and leave to one side to infuse – about 10 minutes will be fine.

In another pan gently melt half the butter and stir in the flour to make a *roux* (a thick creamy paste). Take off the heat and slowly add the cooled milk, stirring all the time to avoid lumps, and allow the sauce to thicken. Return to the heat and gently warm to cook out the flour and let the sauce thicken properly. Stir in the mustard and set aside. If you find that you have any lumps, simply strain the sauce through a sieve.

In a larger pan add the rest of the butter and gently fry the garlic, allowing the butter to become well flavoured. Add all the lobster meat, stirring it around so that it becomes coated in the garlic and butter. Pour in the brandy and set alight until the alcohol is burned off. Pour in the sauce base and add the tarragon. Stir around and season to taste. Place this mixture back in the shells and place under a hot grill for 1-2 minutes until golden on top. Serve. Perfection.

Serves 4

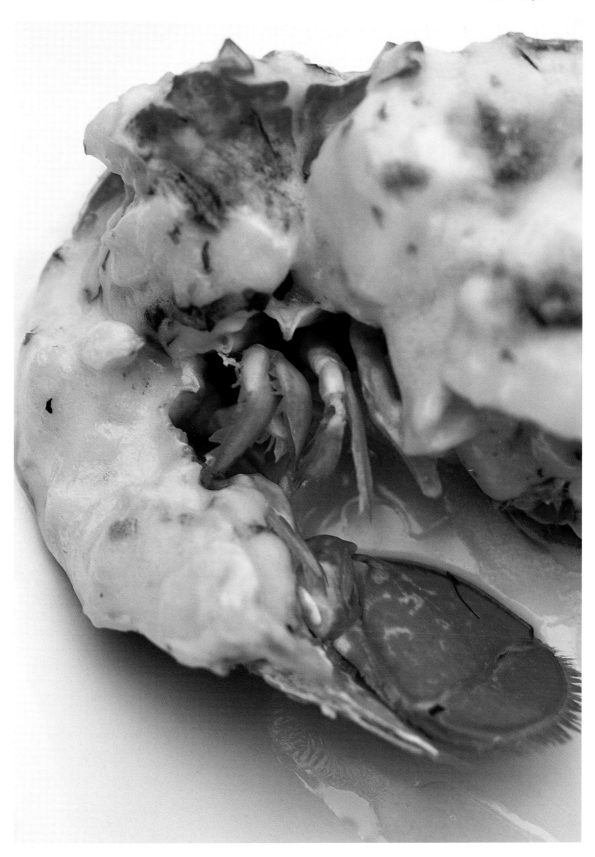

Newlyn Lobster
with Herb and Garlic Mayonnaise

The simpler the better. This shows off lobster perfectly.

2 cooked Newlyn lobsters, 900g/2lb each
150ml/5fl oz aioli (see page 37)
Handful of mixed herbs, including tarragon,
   basil, fennel and parsley

1 lemon
Salad leaves (frisée, rocket, romaine and
   radicchio)
Olive oil

Split the cooked lobsters lengthways and crack the claws. Place half the lobster on each serving plate, cover and keep cool. Mix the aioli, herbs and lemon juice together, then cover and leave in the fridge for 1 hour to allow the flavours to develop.

Serve the lobster with a good dollop of the garlic mayonnaise. Garnish with salad leaves dressed in lemon juice and olive oil.

Serves 4

Lobster Cocktail

I remember prawn cocktails as a luxury. Something to be allowed on Mum's birthday when we went out or at Christmas time when the whole family celebrated together. Nowadays prawns in this country don't seem to taste the same but that's probably nostalgia playing its tricks. To keep the luxurious feel to this dish that I remember from my childhood, I have used freshly boiled lobsters. If you still want to use prawns then look for those which are peeled and packed in brine. They are more expensive than the frozen at sea variety, which I never use, but do have a wonderful firm texture and retain the sweetness of the prawn. At the restaurant we serve these in cocktail glasses which look fabulous with a claw poking through the top of the rich sauce. Try it as a special lunchtime treat in the sun.

2 freshly cooked lobsters, weighing
 600g/1½lb each
½ cup fresh mayonnaise (see page 37)
5 tbsp tomato ketchup
Splash of Worcestershire sauce
Dash of Tabasco

Pinch of cayenne pepper
4 inner leaves of a very fresh cos lettuce (these
 are lighter in colour and sweeter)
Juice of ½ lemon
A few pinches of sea salt

Remove all the meat from the lobster, keeping the claws intact. You do this by splitting the lobster in half and then pulling the meat from the tail and then carefully cracking open the claws and legs. The only thing you need discard from the lobster is the black vein which runs through the tail. This is not always present so don't worry if you can't find it but it will be obvious to you if it is there.

Mix together the mayonnaise, ketchup, Worcestershire sauce, Tabasco and cayenne. Taste. You want all the flavours to be nicely balanced. Finely shred the lettuce and place a small amount in the bottom of each glass. Cover with a tablespoon of the sauce. Put the lobster meat on top, reserving the claw. Cover the lobster with more sauce and then another layer of lettuce. Top off with a small spoonful of sauce and then place a claw on top of each one. Finish with a squeeze of lemon and a pinch of salt.

Serves 4

Try this too...

Lobsters are not always available and can be expensive out of season so try using a mixture of mussels, clams and squid which have been freshly cooked. Bind them with the sauce for a delicious seafood cocktail. Fresh white crab meat lightly bound in the sauce also makes a delicious crab cocktail. If you are an oyster lover then mix 3 or 4 opened oysters with their juice into the sauce and serve in the same way. The possibilities, as with so much fish cooking, are endless.

Lightly Grilled Lobster with Garlic and Herbs

'Lightly grilled' because the lobster is boiled first and therefore doesn't really require any extra cooking, except its fun to have lobster from the barbecue and this is a great way to do it.

1 cooked lobster, about 1kg/2lb
50g/2oz garlic butter (see page 31)
Pinch of sea salt

Juice of $\frac{1}{2}$ lemon
Fresh herbs for garnishing – chives, basil, thyme or chervil and parsley

Split the lobsters in two and remove the meat from the claws and legs. Remove the meat from the tail. Spread garlic butter inside the shell and replace the tail meat. Dot more over the top. Do the same with the head of the fish and then sit the claws on top.

Place under a warm grill or on a hot barbecue shell side down until the butter melts and bubbles. Finish with a sprinkle of sea salt and a squeeze of lemon and garnish with a small bunch of fresh herbs.

Serves 1

Fried Mackerel with Ginger, Garlic and Thyme

An easy lunchtime dish or one to do on the beach when returning from a spot of mackerel fishing.

5g/¼ oz unsalted butter
1 clove of garlic, pasted
25mm/1" piece of root ginger, peeled and
    finely grated

4 large fresh mackerel fillets
Flour
Few springs of thyme
Juice of 1 lime

Heat a pan large enough to take the mackerel fillets, either all together or in pairs. In any case, do not overcrowd the pan. Add the butter, garlic and the ginger and stir so that the butter becomes well flavoured. Give the mackerel a dusting of flour and lay them skin side down in the pan. Cook gently for 3-4 minutes on each side. Remove the mackerel and place on the serving plate.

Add the thyme and the juice of the lime to the pan. Allow to bubble for a few seconds and then spoon over and around the mackerel.

Serves 4

Smoked Mackerel
with Summer Gazpacho and Tarragon Leaf

This is a dish for summer. I usually serve smoked mackerel with salad but here I have used it flaked on top of a rustic chunky gazpacho. It's delicious and full of sunshine flavours.

800g/1¾ lb ripe plum tomatoes, deseeded, peeled and quartered

1 green pepper

1 cucumber, peeled and deseeded

1 mild chilli

275ml/8fl oz good tomato juice

2-3 cloves of garlic

Handful of basil leaves

1 red onion

1 stick of celery

Handful of rocket leaves

2 slices of white bread without crusts

1 tbsp red wine vinegar

4 fillets of smoked mackerel

Tarragon, to garnish

Roughly chop the tomatoes, pepper and cucumber by hand and put into a mixing bowl.

Blend together the chilli, tomato juice, garlic, basil, onion, celery, rocket, the red wine vinegar and bread until smooth and pour over the tomatoes and peppers and season. Leave to chill for a couple of hours and serve in bowls with the mackerel flaked over the top and sprinkled with tarragon leaves.

Serves 4

Poached Mackerel Fillets with Leek, Soft Egg and Anchovy Salad

I love poached fish, especially salmon and mackerel. This salad is a kind of *niçoise* but without any of the traditional ingredients! I suppose it is the inclusion of the egg which makes me think of a *niçoise* – also because I like to serve it as a main course salad and include a few ripe tomatoes, some beans or baby new potatoes. You could add what you like, but start from this and add whatever fresh and seasonal ingredients take your fancy.

For the *court bouillon*
(the liquid in which the fish is poached)

275ml/8fl oz fish stock

1 stick of celery, chopped

Glass of white wine

1 carrot, sliced

1 bay leaf

½ a fennel bulb, sliced

2 mackerel, filleted

2 shallots, finely chopped

For the salad

2 bunches of baby leeks

Squeeze of lemon juice

8 anchovy fillets

Handful of basil, chopped

1 soft boiled egg (about 4 minutes boiling, then into cold water), cut into chunks

For the dressing

Olive oil

Lemon juice

1 tsp of mustard seeds

Pinch of caster sugar

Sea salt and pepper

Put all the ingredients for the *court bouillon* in a pan and bring to the boil. Simmer for 2-3 minutes, take off the heat and leave to infuse while you prepare the salad.

Blanch the leeks for 5 minutes, then drain and cool by dunking into a pan of cold or iced water. Give the leeks a squeeze of lemon to remove any excess water. Place them in a bowl with the anchovies, basil, shallots and roughly chunked egg. Make the dressing by mixing together the oil, salt, lemon, mustard seeds and sugar. Pour over the leeks and finish with black pepper.

Cook the mackerel by bringing the *court bouillon* to a gentle simmer. Add the mackerel and poach lightly for 6-7 minutes. Lift out and serve on a bed of the leek salad.

Serves 2

Sweet and Sour Mackerel

Mackerel must be fresh, a day or two old and not only do they not look as good but they begin to loose their magnificent flavour. Being an oily fish they are recognised as being beneficial for our diets. It's best to catch your own mackerel and cook them on a barbecue within a few hours of being caught. My son Ben and I sat on the quay at Lyme Regis one Fathers' Day and grilled our catch over a disposable barbecue while my daughter Sadie could only look on as a disgruntled non–fish eater, poor thing. This dish is served cold and is popular at FishWorks. We don't do it every day as good, line-caught mackerel supply is sporadic, but when we can we do it and so should you.

25mm/1" root ginger, peeled and finely sliced
1 tsp white peppercorns
4 heads of star anise
1 stalk of celery, finely chopped
1 carrot, peeled and finely sliced
2 shallots, finely sliced
200ml/1/3 pint white wine vinegar

6 tbsp caster sugar
1/2 glass water
2 tbsp Balsamic vinegar
4 sea-fresh mackerel, filleted
Flour for dusting
Handful of fresh coriander, chopped

With the exception of the fish, coriander and flour place all the ingredients in a pan and bring to the boil and simmer for 4-5 minutes. Set aside for 10 minutes to infuse. You are aiming to get a balance between the sour vinegar and the sweet sugar. Dip your finger in; if it is too vinegary then add more sugar, if too sweet, add more vinegar.

Dust the mackerel fillets in flour and fry in a little hot oil, skin side down, for 2-3 minutes then turn over, the skin should be a light golden brown. Place the fish onto a plate and spoon some of the sauce and vegetables over. Lastly, sprinkle with coriander.

Serves 4

Grilled Marlin with Garlic and Caper Mayonnaise

Marlin, sailfish, tuna and swordfish are all readily available at the fishmongers nowadays. Marlin has a white flesh and firm texture and is a delicious game fish suitable for barbecuing and roasting. It works really well on the grill plate and is served here with a sharp garlic and caper mayonnaise. The marlin can be substituted with any other game fish.

150ml/¼ pint vegetable oil
150ml/¼ pint olive oil
2 egg yolks
1 tsp Dijon mustard
1 clove of garlic, pasted with salt

2 tbsp salted capers, rinsed
4 marlin steaks, weighing about 150g/5oz each
Juice of 1 lemon
Sea salt

Make the mayonnaise: mix together the vegetable and olive oils and place the egg yolks into a bowl with the Dijon mustard. Using a hand whisk, gently whisk the egg yolks and mustard together whilst pouring the oil onto the eggs in a gentle, steady stream until a thick emulsion is formed. Add the clove of pasted garlic and the capers and leave in the fridge for an hour or so to allow the flavours to infuse.

Brush the marlin with a little olive oil and grill on a very hot grill plate for 1-2 minutes either side. Serve with a spoonful of the mayonnaise and a handful of green salad leaves. Lastly, as always, finish with a squeeze of lemon and a sprinkling of sea salt.

Serves 4

Try this too...

Add chopped anchovies to the mayonnaise or perhaps a tablespoon of Thai sweet chilli sauce with a handful of coriander.

Monkfish 'Sunday Roast'

I call this a Sunday Roast after the time that I rashly suggested fish for lunch to my family. They were horrified – no joint on a Sunday! So, to convince my sceptical family I realised that I needed something that looked like a joint, something I could stuff with herbs and garlic, that was boneless and could be carved at the table. Basically, something that would fool them.

So, after some thought, large monkfish tails filleted and then tied back together with the thick end of each fillet against the small end of the other one and tied at 25mm/1" intervals was what I came up with eventually. To make it more interesting I made some incisions into the flesh and put slices of garlic, a bit of anchovy and a sprig of rosemary into each one just before roasting. It worked, the family still speak to me and now we sell them over the counter ready prepared at FishWorks.

1 monkfish tail (1kg/2¼lb, filleted)
Small bunch of rosemary
2 cloves of garlic, sliced
6 anchovies
Splash of dry white wine

150ml/¼ pint cream
1 tbsp capers
Juice of 1 lemon
Pinch of sea salt

Ask your fishmonger to fillet the monkfish and remove any membrane on the fish. Then lay the fillets together with the thick end of each fillet against the small end of the other one and tie tightly at 25mm/1" intervals with the string. Next make some incisions randomly in the flesh and insert a piece of garlic, rosemary and anchovy, leaving the rosemary hanging out – do about 10-12 of these – then put the remaining herbs, garlic and anchovies into a roasting tray big enough to take the fish. In a hot pan sear the 'joint' on all sides until golden-brown and transfer to the roasting tray. Add a splash of dry white wine and roast in a hot oven for 10-12 minutes. Remove and rest for a further minute or two to allow the juices to run. Place the monkfish on your best serving plate.

To make the 'gravy', add cream to the roasting pan and bring to the boil, add the capers and lemon juice and pour over the fish. Cut everyone a fillet steak sized chunk and serve with all the trimmings.

Serves 4

Try this too...

If you fancy a change from rosemary, rub the monkfish with a dry mixture of sea salt, lemon zest, garlic and chopped parsley a few hours before roasting, and serve with a spoonful of Salsa Rossa (see page 34) or Hollandaise Sauce (see page 35).

Whole Roasted Peppers
with Monkfish and Rosemary

This is a Mediterranean-style dish which can be eaten hot or cold. I particularly like it as an easy light lunch. You could also serve it cold with the rosemary substituted for fresh basil leaf and a dash of good olive oil.

2 large red peppers
1 clove of garlic, pasted
4 roasted tomatoes (see page 44)
4 fillets of salted anchovies
150ml/5fl oz good olive oil

300g/11oz of monkfish fillet, with the membrane removed and cut into bite-sized chunks
10cm/4" long sprigs of fresh rosemary
Pinch of sea salt
Juice of ½ a lemon

Cut the peppers in half and remove the seeds. Mix together the garlic, roasted tomatoes and anchovy fillet and place equally into the peppers. Pour a few tablespoons of olive oil into each one and roast in a hot oven for 15-20 minutes until the peppers are blackened and softened. Remove them from the oven, place them into a bowl and cover with Clingfilm. This will finish the cooking process and allow the sweet juice of the pepper to run out and be collected in the bowl. This is used afterwards to spoon over and around the pepper when serving.

While the peppers are in the bowl, heat some olive oil in a frying pan until at searing temperature. Fry the monkfish cubes on all sides until golden brown. Add the sprigs of rosemary to the pan and continue to cook for a few minutes so the oil takes on the flavour of the rosemary. The monkfish can then be placed equally into each pepper, the oil spooned on the top and finished with a pinch of sea salt, a squeeze of lemon and garnished with a sprig of rosemary. If you wish to eat them cold just leave them to cool at this stage and add a squeeze more lemon and a sprinkling of sea salt before you serve them.

Serves 4

Try this too...

You can try filling the peppers with freshly cooked mussel meat and chervil; or freshly grilled prawns (with the shell removed) and coriander; or you could just leave them plain with just the tomato and anchovy mix and use them as an accompaniment to a plainly grilled fillet of sea bass or bream.

Pan-fried Monkfish
with Shellfish and Tarragon Sauce

Monkfish has a great texture but the flavour can be lacking slightly when compared to other fish. Here, the flavour of the tarragon mixing with the cockles and shellfish really lifts the flavour of the dish. It's ideal for the shellfish addict as well as nervous fish eaters (there are no bones). Use whatever shellfish is available.

2 tomatoes, skinned and diced	8 mussels
Fresh tarragon, chopped	12 clams
Olive oil	12 winkles
600g/1¼ lb monkfish fillet	150ml/5fl oz cream
1-2 cloves of garlic	Butter
Splash of white wine	400g/14oz spinach
2 handfuls of live cockles, in the shell	Salt and pepper

Preheat the oven to 400°F/200°C/gas mark 6. Heat the olive oil in a good pan until hot. Season the fish with salt and pepper and place in the pan. Cook until golden (this should only take a few minutes). Turn the fish over and repeat. Take the pan off the heat and pop the whole thing into the oven for 2 minutes.

Take another pan, add a little oil and sweat a clove or so of garlic. Add a generous splash of wine, boil for 1 minute then add the shellfish and allow to steam open discarding any that don't. Add the cream, the tomatoes and the tarragon. Take off the heat and put aside.

In a third pan, gently sweat the spinach with a decent sized piece of butter and season.

Lay the spinach in the centre of the bowl, place the fish on top and spoon the sauce and shellfish around the edible island.

Serves 4

Red Mullet with Greek Salad

Red mullet is such a beautiful looking fish. When just caught they have a wonderful deep red colour with a white belly and a distinct yellow line running down the side. After a few days this colour and radiance fades to a dull pink, so it is easy to tell a fresh mullet, it will jump out at you on any good fishmonger's display. They are extremely popular around the Mediterranean and I have spent many balmy nights picking over a fresh grilled mullet with a bowl of salad or a fresh local vegetable and a few bottles of chilled wine. Here I have put a Greek salad with the fish. The combination of salty cheese, olives and fruity oil are a perfect foil for sweet, grilled mullet.

2 red mullet weighing around 250g/9oz each, scaled and gutted
Good olive oil
Juice of 1 lemon
Good pinch of dried oregano
Tbsp fresh mint, chopped
6 leaves from a round lettuce

3 ripe tomatoes, cut into quarters
$1/4$ whole cucumber, cut in half lengthways and sliced
1 small red onion, finely sliced
$1/2$ handful of black olives, preferably Kalamata
100g/4oz good quality feta cheese
Pinch of sea salt

Brush the mullet with olive oil and place under a hot grill for 3 minutes then place in a hot oven for a further 5 minutes.

Make the dressing by mixing the oil, lemon juice and herbs together well. Toss this with the remaining ingredients and place on a plate. When the mullet is cooked lay this alongside the salad and finish with a drizzle of olive oil.

Serves 2

Grey Mullet Baked with Ginger and Green Onions

My first experience of ginger with steamed fish was in a local Chinese restaurant in my youth and since that day I have often cooked similar dishes at home. This version works perfectly and recreates that initial eating experience extremely well.

I have used grey mullet because I think it is underrated as a fish and can often be found at a very reasonable price on your fishmonger's slab. When buying grey mullet ask your fishmonger if the fish was sea-caught or from an estuary. You will find that estuarine fish have a slightly muddier flavour than those caught out at sea. Either way they are both good and not to be missed when in prime fresh condition.

25mm/1" of fresh ginger, skinned and
   finely grated
1 clove of garlic, finely sliced
1 shallot, finely sliced
3 spring onions, cut into fine strips or chunks,
   cut at an angle across the onion
2 tbsp of light soy sauce
1 tsp of Shaoxxing white wine or dry sherry

3 tbsp water
Allow 1 grey mullet weighing 450g/1lb per
   person (ask your fishmonger to remove the
   scales and gut – the head can be left on or off,
   as your prefer)
Squeeze of lime juice
Handful of fresh chopped coriander, including
   the root

Lay the fish on a square of tin foil large enough to completely wrap the fish and form a tight seal. Mix together all of the ingredients with the exception of the lime juice and coriander. Pour over the fish and seal the tin foil by rolling over the edges together and crimping with your fingers. Ensure there is no room for any liquid to escape. Carefully pick up the parcels, place them on a roasting tray and into a pre-heated oven, as hot as you can get, and place on the middle shelf for around 20 minutes.

Remove each parcel carefully from the oven, remembering that they will be very hot, and place un-opened onto a serving plate. Open the top of each parcel, add a squeeze of lime juice and a sprinkle of coriander, and serve.

Serves 1

This dish is wonderful eaten with a cold noodle salad. Just cook noodles, wash and drain and set aside. Mix 6 tablespoons of lime juice, 6 tablespoons of water with 1 tablespoon of caster sugar and chopped chilli until the sugar has dissolved. Toss with the noodles (you could also add some cooked prawns here) and finish with some sesame seeds.

Curried Mussel Soup with Coriander Leaf

An easy and successful way of bringing out the very best in mussels.

3kg/6½ lb live mussels
⅓ bottle dry white wine
40g/1½ oz unsalted butter
1 leek, finely chopped
1 onion, chopped
3 celery sticks, chopped
3 cloves of garlic, chopped

1 tbsp curry powder
2 sprigs of fresh thyme
1l/1¾ pints fish stock
2 large potatoes
35ml/1½ fl oz double cream
Handful of coriander, chopped

Steam the mussels open in a little white wine and cool. Remove the meat from the shells and strain the cooking juices and set aside.

Melt the butter in a pan and add the vegetables and cook gently until softened. Add the curry powder and thyme and cook for a further 5 minutes. Add the stock and potatoes and cook for a further 15 minutes. Finally add the whole mussels, the juices and double cream and then liquidise.

To finish, pass the soup through a sieve to strain and then serve piping hot with a sprinkling of chopped coriander leaf.

Serves 4

Baked Mussels
with Roasted Peppers, Aioli and Basil

This dish makes a great starter or even rather flamboyant nibbles for a drinks party. They can also be eaten cold and prepared in advance, apart from the final topping.

1 red pepper
1 yellow pepper
400g/14oz mussels per person

Aioli (see page 37)
Handful of basil leaves, shredded

Place the peppers on a roasting tray and sprinkle with a little olive oil and salt. Roast in a hot oven for 25 minutes and remove. Place into a container and cover with Clingfilm for a further 20 minutes. When they are cooled remove the seeds and charred skin and chop into fine dice.

Steam the mussels open in a little water and remove the opened shell to leave the mussel meat in the half shell.

Make the aioli which can be made the day before and kept in the fridge to allow the flavours to develop.

To assemble the dish, warm the mussels through under a grill for 1 minute. Place on a plate and top with a teaspoon of peppers, some aioli and a pinch of the shredded basil.

Serves 4

Steamed Mussels Marinière

Everyone enjoys a bowl of steaming mussels. They should be fat, juicy and smothered in heaps of garlic and fresh parsley. I have seen cream added to the sauce but I prefer them plain and simple in their own juices. Personally, I enjoy them served with a bowl of aioli on the table, some good hard crusted fresh bread and an endless supply of chilled wine.

Olive oil
2 cloves of garlic, finely chopped
1 shallot, finely chopped
Glass of dry white wine

Allow 600g/1¼ lb mussels per person as a
  main course
Handful of parsley leaf, chopped

Gently sweat the garlic and shallots in the olive oil until softened. Do not brown. Add the wine, boil for a minute, and then add the mussels. Replace the lid, and cook, giving it a shake from time to time. The mussels are ready when they have opened – be sure to discard any that don't. Spoon the mussels into a serving bowl then add the parsley to the pan, give it a stir and pour over the mussels.

Serves 1

Mussel, Clam and Leek Stew with Aioli

Mussels and clam beds are plentiful around the British shoreline and the coast of Brittany. Inside these seashells the delicious sweet meat of each mollusc is kept fresh in seawater. The golden rule for clams and mussels? If it's shut tight when it's cooked then don't eat it, put it straight in the bin. After all, there are plenty more fish in the sea....

Pinch of saffron
2 egg yolks
3 cloves of garlic, pasted
150ml/5fl oz olive oil
1 shallot, finely chopped
2 leeks, cut into thin chunks
1 glass of white wine

450g/1lb fresh, live mussels, cleaned
    and scrubbed
200g/7oz clams
Few sprigs of fresh thyme
600ml/1 pint fish stock
Salt and pepper

There are many variations of aioli that you could make. I find that this one works superbly with fish. Any that is leftover will keep in the fridge for 3-4 days. To make, steep the saffron in a little hot water and then place in a bowl with the egg yolks and garlic. Whisk these together and gradually, whilst still whisking, gently pour in the olive oil (in a steady trickle) until an emulsion is formed and the mixture has thickened.

Gently fry the shallots, garlic and leek in a little olive oil until softened. Add the white wine and boil for a minute to remove some of the alcohol. Add the mussels, clams, fresh thyme and fish stock. Cover the pan. Allow the stew to steam for around 4 minutes, or until the mussels and clams are open.

To serve, divide the shellfish into 2 bowls and pour over the juices. Top with a generous tablespoonful of aioli. Good olive bread accompanies this well, as does an enormous glass of good dry white wine.

Serves 2

Menorcan Octopus

I first ate this dish in a wonderful restaurant in Menorca called, appropriately, Polpo. This is a typical Spanish dish eaten throughout the coastal towns of Spain. I love its sheer simplicity, and it was just perfect eaten under the setting sun overlooking the vivid blue Mediterranean with my children, Sadie and Ben. I don't think we eat enough octopus, perhaps because we are scared of it. This is probably the only recipe that I would agree to using frozen octopus as the freezing process tenderises it without the need for bashing with a mallet. Also the octopus we get off of the British coast are quite small and this is a recipe that calls for large thick tentacles. Frozen octopus tend to come from Japan or Africa and are much larger and come ready cleaned. Octopus seems to need either a lot of cooking or very little – it seems anything in between just doesn't work. In this recipe the octopus is just dipped in boiling water for a few minutes, three times. When I asked the waiter at Polpo how mine was cooked he said the chef 'scares' it. A nice phrase to describe this unusual technique.

200g/7oz octopus tentacles
Sea salt
Handful of parsley, chopped

Squeeze of lemon juice
Good olive oil for drizzling

First rub the octopus with salt.

Bring a pan of water to the boil and with a pair of tongs plunge the octopus into the water for about 40 seconds. Pull it out for 10 seconds and do the same again twice more. Allow to cool and then thinly slice at an angle across the tentacle and place in a single layer on a plate – in Spain they use a wooden board. Sprinkle with parsley, a squeeze of lemon and a good soaking of good olive oil.

Serves 4 as a starter or a tapa

Crisp-fried Plaice with Chilli and Coriander Jam

Fish fried in good crumb batter can either be delicious or a soggy disaster. But when it works it is a real gastronomic treat. This is great finger food and the coriander 'jam' is so versatile it is one of those things you should make up in advance and keep in the fridge. I sometimes find myself spreading it on sandwiches or adding a tablespoon to a bowl of mussels. It is based on Thai sweet chilli sauce which is worth having in your store cupboard if you're feeling lazy but here I wanted to try and make it completely fresh. After a bit of chatting with my colleague Matthew Prouse, our head chef at Bristol FishWorks, this is what we came up with.

2 large plaice, filleted and skinned
2 tbsp flour

1 egg, beaten
Handful of Japanese panko breadcrumbs

For the jam
5-6 large chillies, mild
600g/1¼lb ripe tomatoes
75g/3oz fresh root ginger, peeled and chopped
50ml/2fl oz Thai fish sauce
5 cloves of garlic, peeled

150ml/5fl oz red wine vinegar
450g/1lb caster sugar
Handful of fresh coriander
Juice of 1 lime
Lime wedges to serve

Cut the plaice into long strips about 25mm/1" wide. Dip them first into flour, then beaten egg and then breadcrumbs and lay on a plate ready for frying. Pop in the fridge until needed.

To make the jam blend together the chillis, whole tomatoes, including the skin and seeds, ginger, fish sauce and garlic into a purée. Add this to the vinegar and sugar in a saucepan and slowly bring to the boil, stirring frequently, removing any scum that may come to the surface. Cook for 30-40 minutes stirring frequently until a 'jam' consistency is reached. Before serving add the coriander and lime juice.

Cook the plaice by deep-frying until crisp and golden in hot oil heated to a temperature of 325°F/170°C. This will take about 4-5 minutes. Serve on a plate with a wedge of lime and a dollop of chilli jam.

Serves 4

Try this too...

Instead of plaice, use fresh prawns or try the chilli jam with fresh barbecued mackerel. It is also good stirred into a wok when frying crisp vegetables and excellent when used for basting octopus or squid on the barbecue.

Char-grilled Prawns
with Lime, Chilli, Red Onion and Parsley Leaf

I think this dish makes a wonderful starter. It can be eaten in the depths of winter to remind you of the forthcoming summer or eaten in the garden on a hot, sunny afternoon either straight from the barbecue in big bowls for everybody to dig into or on individual plates. The colours in the dish look magnificent while the succulent prawns taste just delicious, having a slightly charred flavour from the grill.

Ask your fishmonger for king prawns with a 16-20 count – these represent a good size and what it means is there are 16-20 prawns to the kilo. They are available in a 12 count, and the giants 6-8; so for a celebration, treat everybody to the 6-8's.

16 large prawns with the shell on, with the head
  on or off, as you prefer
Juice of 2 limes
1 red onion, finely chopped

Good handful of flat parsley leaf, chopped
2 mild chillies, finely chopped
Sprinkling of sea salt
Olive oil

Split the prawns down the back using a small, sharp knife. If you are using prawns with the head on start at the bottom of the head and make a cut right through to the tail so that the body is completely cut in half. If you are using prawns without the head, make a cut from the top to the tail but keeping the tail intact. Mix together all of the ingredients and allow to marinate in the fridge for a minimum of 4 hours.

When you are ready to cook, place the prawns on the barbecue or grill. Because of the oil in the marinade it will probably smoke and flame, so if you are cooking on an outside grill just spray some cold water on the coals to cool them down and if you are cooking inside make sure there is a window open! Cook the prawns for 2 minutes either side turning with some tongs. The dark shell will start to turn red taking on the flavour of the hot grill while the meat of the prawn cooks with the flavour of the marinade.

Remove them from the grill, add a further squeeze of lime, a sprinkling of sea salt and sprinkle some finely chopped parsley over the top. Serve this with crusty bread and a glass of crisp, dry wine. Make sure your guests have plenty of napkins on the table and a bowl of warm water to wash their fingers. If you are using whole prawns make sure everybody sucks the head once they have broken it from the body of the prawn as this contains delicious dark meat.

Serves 4

Grilled Razor Clams
with Parsley, Lemon and Garlic

You don't see razor clams very often but if you do they are an absolute must to buy. As with all shellfish they must be bought live and this is easy to check as often they hang from the end of their long thin shells almost waving at you. When picked up or touched they quickly retract back inside their shell. They certainly look strange, but don't be put off as they taste delicious and the simplicity and speed of this recipe makes it superb for any occasion.

16 razor clams

Olive oil

2 cloves of garlic, pasted

Splash of white wine

Couple of handfuls of fresh breadcrumbs

Juice of 1 lemon

Handful of flatleaf parsley, chopped

Butter

Thoroughly wash the razor clams to remove any grit from the outside and the ends of the shells. Do not leave them soaking in fresh water for any length of time as this will kill them as they are used to life in salt water.

In a large pan, big enough to hold the clams, gently sweat the garlic in a little olive oil to flavour and then add a splash of wine and the clams. Place the lid on and cook over a high heat until the clams have just opened. Discard those which do not open. Remove the clams from the pan and place 4 in a row, with the open side facing upwards, on each plate.

Add the breadcrumbs, parsley and lemon juice to the juices in the pan, heat through and spoon over each clam. Dot some small chunks of butter over each clam and place under the grill for 2-3 minutes until the butter has melted into the breadcrumbs. Finish with a final sprinkling of parsley and a further squeeze of lemon.

Serves 4

Try this too...

This recipe works equally well with mussels, cockles or any other clam.

Roasted Salmon
with Salsa Picante and Coriander

This Salsa Picante is really just a hot Mexican sauce. I love the seeds in it and the fresh zing of lime and coriander and it really does work well with salmon, which so often nowadays needs a little lift. I wouldn't, however, dream of doing anything else with a piece of wild salmon other than poaching it and eating it warm with Hollandaise Sauce (see page 35) or cold with Mayonnaise (see page 37).

Handful of pumpkin seeds
1 tsp sesame seeds
$1/2$ tsp cumin seeds
4 roasted tomatoes (see page 44)
6 tbsp cider vinegar
Handful of fresh coriander

Juice of 1 lime
3 whole hot chillies, seeds removed
1 tbsp dried oregano
4 cloves of garlic
4 pieces of salmon fillet weighing about
   150g/5oz each

Make the salsa by toasting the seeds until golden in a heavy based frying pan. Add to a food processor and then pile in all the other ingredients, except the salmon. Whiz making sure that you don't overdo it – you need a roughly chopped feel.

Sear the salmon in a hot pan until golden and then finish cooking in a hot oven for a further 4-5 minutes until just pink on the inside. Serve with a spoonful of the sauce, a wedge of lime and a sprig of coriander.

Serves 4

Penne with Sardines

Sardines are such a versatile and delicious fish. Even good tinned sardines in tomato sauce with a dried chilli and handfuls of fresh coriander makes for a simple quick sauce for pasta or a topping for toast or little rounds of grilled ciabatta as crostini. But, of course, very fresh sardines are the best of all. This is a dish you might find in Sicily. I imagine it being cooked up in a small, homely kitchen with a few kilos of the day's catch. If you happen to see some stunningly fresh sardines then treat friends and family to a big bowl in the middle of the table served with lots of chilled white Corvo.

400g/14oz penne
Good olive oil
1 onion, chopped
6 sardines, filleted
2 tbsp currants

1 tbsp pine nuts
Pinch of nutmeg
Handful of basil leaves
Sea salt and pepper
Squeeze of lemon juice

Cook your pasta.

Meanwhile, gently fry the onion in olive oil, adding a little water to moisten. While you are doing this, lightly oil the sardine fillets and grill skin side down until the skin is charred and crisp. This will add an almost 'outdoor' flavour to the dish. Remove from the grill and add to the onions. Add the currants, pine nuts and nutmeg and continue to stir. Don't worry if the fish breaks up.

Just before tossing with the pasta, season the sauce with crunchy sea salt, a turn of black pepper and finally add the basil and lemon juice. If the sauce appears a little dry add a tablespoon or two of water or a glug of good olive oil. Toss with the pasta and serve.

Serves 4

Sardines on Toast

We've all eaten them. Rich tinned sardines mashed on to thick buttery toast and finished with a squeeze of lemon and a sprinkling of fresh basil or parsley. But how many of us have tried fresh sardines on toast? I think they make one of the most simple yet delicious dishes I know. That doesn't mean there is anything wrong with tinned ones. I often open a tin and stir them into pasta with fresh herbs or, back to the best way, sevred on toast.

4 slices of ciabatta	3 basil leaves, shredded
Good olive oil	2 plump sardines, filleted
1 clove of garlic	Juice of 1/2 lemon
2 tomatoes, roughly chopped	Pinch of sea salt
2 black olives, finely chopped	

Brush the bread with olive oil and grill until just golden on the barbecue. When slightly cooled rub with a cut garlic clove on both sides.

Mix together the tomatoes, olives and basil and spoon onto the bread. Brush the sardines with oil and grill skin side down for 2-3 minutes until just cooked. Then place one on each piece of bread and finish with a squeeze of lemon and a pinch of crunchy sea salt.

Serves 2

Cured Sardines with Fresh Parsley and Garlic

I usually do this with fresh anchovies but sardines are more readily available and work just as well. Try and buy smaller fish. They make a great communal starter, just a big plate of these and a few glasses of wine gets everyone going.

12 very fresh sardines, filleted
2 cloves of garlic, finely chopped
150ml/¼ pint good olive oil

Few pinches of sea salt
150ml/¼ pint white wine vinegar
Handful of parsley, chopped

Genly warm the olive oil to body temperature and add the garlic. Leave to infuse for 20 minutes. Then add the vinegar and give a good stir.

Lay the sardines on a non-metallic tray and sprinkle with sea salt, then pour over the oil and vinegar mixture making sure the fish is well coated. Leave overnight in the fridge and finish with a good sprinkling of parsley before serving.

Try this too...

Barbecue or shallow fry the sardines before curing and change the parsley for coriander or thyme.

Sea Scallops with a Garlic Glaze

Good scallops are so sweet they hardly need cooking. And the simpler the method the better. When buying, ask your fishmonger for hand dived scallops. They will cost more but you won't regret it.

250g/9oz butter, melted
3 cloves of garlic, pasted
2 egg yolks
Juice of 1 lemon
1 tbsp tarragon, chopped

1 tbsp parsley, chopped
12 scallops with bottom shells
Olive oil
Sea salt

First make the glaze. Melt the butter and garlic together and season. Allow to sit and infuse for 20 minutes in a heatproof bowl. Whisk the egg yolks with a teaspoon of cold water until light and bubbly over a pan of boiling water – this will take about 2-3 minutes. Be careful not to scramble the eggs. Remove from the heat and in a steady stream, whilst whisking, add the melted butter and garlic until the sauce thickens. Then add the lemon juice and herbs and leave to one side.

Next, brush the scallops with olive oil and a sprinkling of salt, sear on either side in a pre-heated dry frying pan for 1-2 minutes. Place back into the shells, coat with the sauce and finally put under a hot – and I mean hot – grill, to glaze the top of the sauce.

Serves 2

Scallop and Tabbouleh Salad

I first had Tabbouleh at a barbecue some years ago prepared by some Iranian friends. It looked so colourful and the parsley and lemon juice which was abundant in it tasted so fresh. I made some the next day and then just seared a few slices of scallops and threw them in – it was easy and tasted great. Tabbouleh is a salad of which the main ingredient is bulghar wheat. Lee, one of the chefs at our Bristol restaurant, recently introduced me to a grain called ebley which he used in this dish. It was slighlty larger than bulghar and almost gelatinous in texture. I had never come across it before and now prefer it. That's the great thing about cooking, you never stop learning.

200g/7oz bulghar wheat or ebley
Pinch of sea salt
Good handful of parsley, chopped
Handful of mint, chopped
Small bunch of spring onions, sliced
Zest of 1 lemon
4 tomatoes, seeds removed and the flesh
  cut into small dice
¼ cucumber, de-seeded and cut into small dice
1 clove of garlic, pasted
Juice of 2 lemons
Good quality olive oil
8 good-sized scallops, cut in half cross-ways

Soak the bulghar wheat for 10 minutes in cold water then drain. Put into a pan with 375ml/13fl oz cold water, add a pinch of salt and simmer for 20 minutes until all the water is absorbed and leave to cool.

Mix together the wheat, parsley, mint, spring onions, lemon zest, tomato and cucumber. In a separate bowl whisk together the garlic, lemon juice and olive oil and mix into the salad.

Brush the scallops with oil and sear in a pan for no more than a minute each side until just golden. Using your hands, stir the scallops gently into the salad making sure all the ingredients are evenly distributed. Serve in a large bowl in the middle of the table.

Serves 4

Scallops with Pancetta

Pancetta is a smoked Italian bacon, which is now widely available in Britain. The wonderful smoky flavour of the pancetta really enhances the natural sweetness of the scallops. However, if you can't get hold of any pancetta you could replace it with good quality smoked bacon. The simple butter, lemon and thyme sauce brings the whole dish together. This is a dish that needs to be cooked moments before it is eaten, so you can't prepare it in advance, but it is so simple that you'll be able to produce it in minutes – great as a starter or a light lunch.

Small salad leaves
Lemon juice
Olive oil
200g/7oz pancetta, cut into lardons
   (little rectangles)

20 scallops removed from shell
   (dived not dredged)
75g/3oz unsalted butter
Fresh thyme or lemon thyme
1 lemon

Dress your salad leaves with good olive oil and a little lemon juice. You'll add this to each serving plate at the last moment.

Get your large frying pan really hot, add a glug of olive oil and fry the pancetta until really crisp. Remove the pancetta from the pan and scatter equally over the serving plates. Add the scallops to the hot pan and sear each side for 1-2 minutes. Remove the scallops from the pan and place five on each plate in a circle. Quickly add the butter to the pan until it is just bubbling, then add the thyme, a pinch of sea salt and the juice of the lemon. Now spoon this sauce over the scallops and place a handful of dressed salad leaves in the centre of the plate.

Serves 4

Pan-fried Scallops with Sauce Vierge

Sauce Vierge is an olive-oil-based sauce enlivened with fresh summery herbs and tomatoes. Here it is used with scallops but would work with most other fish. The only fish I don't use it with is those of the oily variety like mackerel and herring.

24 scallops out of shell, corals removed	1 large tomato, skinned and roughly chopped
150ml/5fl oz olive oil	1 clove of garlic, crushed
Salt and pepper	1 lemon
Coriander seeds	Fresh basil

Brush the scallops with a little olive oil then season them with salt and pepper. Crush a few coriander seeds in a pestle and mortar (the flavour is strong so a little goes a long way). Heat a dry pan until very hot and sear the scallops on each side for 1-2 minutes, if your pan has a metal handle be very careful not to burn your hand. Arrange 6 scallops on each plate.

Warm the remaining oil in a pan and add the coriander seeds, tomato and garlic. Stir in the lemon juice and shredded basil, then spoon the oil over the scallops. A few basil sprigs make an attractive and appropriate garnish.

Serves 4

Grilled Shark with Garlic and Green Peppercorns

Shark has a lovely, meaty, gelatinous texture and when bought fresh is wonderful lightly grilled or stewed. Shark can, however, be unpleasant if old. When buying check that the colour is pale and creamy and with no aroma. You will instantly know when the shark has 'turned' as it will smell of ammonia. The best kind of eating shark is porbeagle which is caught through the summer months off the Cornish coast. There are also wonderful shark loins which are imported from the Far East and Sri Lanka and will always be reasonably priced in comparison to say tuna, swordfish or marlin, all of which can act as substitutes, if shark is not available.

1 tbsp green peppercorns, preferably those in brine
3 cloves of garlic, pasted
Pinch of saffron
Juice of 1/2 a lemon

Handful of fresh parsley, chopped
150ml/5fl oz of good olive oil
600g/1 1/4 lb piece of shark loin, cut into 25mm/1" cubes

First make the dressing, which also acts as a marinade in this dish, by blitzing together the green peppercorns, garlic, parsley, saffron, lemon zest and olive oil. Spoon over the shark so that it is covered well and leave in the fridge to marinate for at least 1-2 hours.

Pre-heat the grill or barbecue and place the shark pieces on or under the grill for 2-3 minutes either side until nicely charred and just cooked through. Place them on a plate with a squeeze of lemon and the remaining marinade and accompany with a salad of sliced tomato, red onion, coriander and lime juice.

Serves 4

Try this too...

Shark is wonderful for fish curry and can be marinated in commercially bought tandoori paste or used in a green curry with green curry paste, fresh ginger, coconut milk, noodles and fresh coriander.

Brown Shrimp Omelette

Eggs and fish – my two favourite things. A creamy omelette with sweet brown shrimps or perhaps crab or lobster meat with tarragon is hard to beat for a simple indulgent supper. If you really want to indulge and remind yourself that food is one of life's greatest pleasures then try dolloping a tablespoon of caviar on top of a soft boiled egg and watch those little black eggs mix with the creamy yolk. My friend, Martin Blunos, at his two Michelin-star restaurant Lettonie in Bath, takes this simplicity to its heights by scrambling duck eggs perfectly, popping them back in their shell and covering the top with Sevruga Caviar. He makes the occasion even more special as he serves it on a stand, pours vodka on the plate and then sets fire to it which just finishes flaming as the eggs arrive at the table amidst a fantastic glowing blue flame. All washed down with a glass of his homemade flavoured vodka. So there, fish and eggs, luxurious and indulgent.

25g/1oz of butter
6 large eggs, lightly whisked
100g/4oz peeled brown shrimps
Pinch of mace

1 tsp of chervil, chopped
Small squeeze of lemon
Salt and pepper

Make sure you have a good non-stick pan, it makes the job much easier. Melt half the butter in a pan, season the eggs and pour in half of them, tilt the pan so they touch the sides and cook over a gentle heat.

In a separate pan melt the remaining butter and add the shrimps and mace and gently warm for 1-2 minutes. As the omelette is setting, add the chervil and lemon to the shrimps, and pour over the top of the omelette. Add a turn of black pepper and finish under the grill. Slide out of the pan onto your plate and cook the other in the same way, keeping your hands off the first one!

Serves 2

Grilled Skate with Mustard, Red Chicory and Fennel

This is a dish for the summer. The accompanying salad of crunchy fennel and slightly bitter red chicory goes splendidly with any grilled or roasted fish and shellfish.

4 skate wings weighing 250g/9oz each
50g/2oz unsalted butter
4 heads of chicory (use green if red is
not available)
4 heads of fennel
Handful of rocket leaves

For the dressing
3 tbsp apple juice or dry cider
1 tsp chopped tarragon leaves
1 egg yolk
Juice of 1/2 lemon
2 tsp grain or Dijon mustard
150ml/5fl oz olive oil

Spread the skate liberally with the softened butter and place under a hot grill for 5-6 minutes and then place in a hot oven to finish cooking for a further 5 minutes.

While the skate is cooking, make the salad by breaking the chicory into pieces by pulling the leaves outwardly from the base. Then chop the roots from the fennel and slice very finely, preferably on a mandolin. Be sure to include the nice feathery fronds form the top of the bulb. Then place the fennel, chicory and rocket in a bowl.

For the dressing place the egg yolk, mustard and lemon juice into your blender and blitz to a smooth paste. Gradually drizzle in the olive oil in a steady stream untill a thick emulsion is formed. Then add the cider or apple juice, which will loosen the sauce and create a frothy finish. If still a little thick, add a tablespoon of cold water. The dressing should be creamy and light with a layer of bubbles on the top. Finally add a teaspoon of chopped tarragon and amalgamate with the dressing. Dress the salad and serve on a plate, next to the skate.

Serves 4

Pan-fried Skate with Capers and Black Butter

This is a classic way of cooking skate. I love black butter so I never confine it just to skate. It works well with sole and especially plaice.

New potatoes	1 tsp red wine vinegar
Olive oil for frying	1 tbsp capers
2 skate wings	1 lemon
Unsalted butter	Fresh parsley

Bring a pan of salted water to the boil. Add the new potatoes to the water and cook until tender. Start the potatoes a few minutes before the fish. This should be done in the time it takes to cook the skate.

Heat the olive oil in a pan until hot. Add the skate wings, one by one, and fry until golden for about 1-2 minutes, then turn them over and repeat. Place the whole pan into a hot oven to finish cooking for 6-7 minutes. (Choose a pan with a metal handle, not plastic, and don't pick it up with bare hands once it's hot.) Once the wings are cooked, remove them from the pan and place onto serving plates.

Add a generous piece of butter to the pan, stir in the wine vinegar, and continue to cook until the butter starts to brown. Add the capers, squeeze in the lemon juice and finally add the chopped parsley to the pan. Pour your butter sauce over the skate and serve with the new potatoes and a very satisfied look on your face.

Serves 2

Grilled Skate with Savoy Cabbage and Parsley Sauce

This dish is a bit like cod with parsley sauce, it just works. Try and buy large, fat skate wings but where skate isn't available ask for blonde ray. Skate is rarely available these days and so at FishWorks we often buy other species of ray – they are just as good but the blonde ray is my favourite, it has bigger wings and the flesh is much meatier.

Make sure the skate is already skinned when you buy it because I can assure you that unless you have the strength of Goliath and have developed the technique you will not be able to remove the skin at home!

4 skate wings, or 2 larger ones cut in half
   (skate portions about 250-275g/9-10oz each)
50g/2oz butter, softened
Béchamel sauce, enough for 4 (see page 36)

1 clove of garlic, pasted
200g/7oz Savoy cabbage, finely shredded
Sea salt
Juice of 1 lemon

Place each skate wing on a roasting tray which will fit under your grill and rub liberally with a coating of softened butter. Place the skate under the grill for 5-6 minutes, the butter will add a lovely golden colour to the skate. Finally place the skate in the roasting tray in a hot oven for a further 5 minutes.

In the meantime, warm through your parsley sauce base and add handfuls of fresh chopped parsley.

In a separate pan gently melt the rest of the butter, add the garlic and gently cook the cabbage (try to use a mixture of the darker outer leaves and the sweeter inner leaves) until softened, and finish with a sprinkling of sea salt.

To serve, place the skate on the middle of the plate, pour the parsley sauce over and around and spoon a pile of cabbage over the thick end of the skate wing.

Serves 4

Red Snapper Baked in Coconut Milk with Galangal, Lime Leaves, Chillies and Green Coriander

This dish is based upon Thai ingredients all of which are now readily available in good supermarkets or Asian stores. It is typical of Thai food in that it just has bags and bags of flavour. The other thing about this dish is that it is all cooked in one pot which leaves you free to enjoy your guests' company.

3 x 400ml/12fl oz tins of coconut milk
2 tbsp sugar syrup or 1 tbsp caster sugar
2 tsp nam pla (a fish sauce available in oriental food stores)
3 cloves of garlic, crushed
15mm/¾" piece of ginger, finely grated
3 roots of fresh galangal, shredded
Generous handful of lime leaves, finely shredded

2 sticks of lemon grass, crushed and split open
4 spring onions, trimmed and left whole
1 large bunch of fresh coriander, torn roughly, plus extra to garnish
2-5 birds eye chillies, according to taste, split open
4 red snapper fillets, or whole fish, scaled and gutted

Pre-heat the oven to 425°F/220°C/gas mark 7. Put the coconut milk, syrup or sugar and fish sauce into a deep sided ovenproof casserole dish. Add all the other ingredients apart from the fish. Mix well, then gently immerse the fish – the coconut milk mixture should just cover about two thirds of the fish. Cover with a lid or foil and bake in the oven for 15 minutes. Serve straight from the oven, garnish with more coriander and serve with jasmine rice and steamed oriental leaves.

Serves 4

Dover Sole with Brown Shrimps and Parsley Leaf

Sweet peeled brown shrimp, or *crevette grisse* as they are known in France, add something special to this dish. I like to eat the shells on the shrimp, so I leave them on and cook them whole. If, however, you prefer peeled then they can be. Dover sole are poor value for money between the months of January and mid-April when they are heavily in roe. The summer months are the best time for this magnificent fish, and a fish weighing 450-500gms/14-16oz will make a fine meal for one.

1 450g/1lb sole   Butter
A handful of shrimps

For the parsley sauce
75g/3oz butter   Juice of 1 lemon
Pinch of crunchy sea salt   Handful of parsley, chopped

Place the sole on a grill or roasting tray and spread liberally with softened butter and pop under a pre-heated grill for 6-7 minutes until the skin starts to crisp and the butter becomes golden. Then place in a hot oven for a further 6-7 minutes to finish cooking.

While the sole is in the oven place the butter in a pan over a gentle heat, melting it until it starts to foam. You will notice it start to turn a light brown colour and begin to smell nutty. You have made *noissette* butter! At this stage remove from the heat, add the sea salt, and squeeze the lemon. Be very careful as this will spit and steam when the cold lemon juice mixes with the butter. Add the chopped parsley, which will further crackle and spit. Have a taste – it should be sharp and fresh tasting and non-oily. Place the whole fish on the plate and spoon 2-3 table-spoons of your butter over the back of the fish.

Add the shrimps at the same time as the parsley sauce and spoon over the cooked sole.

Grilled Sole with Lemon and Parsley Butter

The best sole of all is, of course, the magnificent Dover. However, fish such as megrim, which are caught off the Scilly Isles, lemon sole, witch sole and small sand soles, which resemble the Dover sole and are often half the price, are delicious to eat just simply grilled as in this recipe. The key point, as with all of the other dishes I have chosen for this book, is freshness. I like to serve sole on the bone – I think they look spectacular on the plate and the bones help in keeping the fish moist whilst cooking. I also think it makes more of an occasion when, after eating the thick top fillet on the sole, you are able to pick through the edge of the bone and in between the fins for those lovely crispy, gelatinous pieces of flesh. If you are using Dover sole ask your fishmonger to skin them as their skin is particularly tough and not suitable for this dish. The other soles I have mentioned have thinner skins and are really good to eat – attempting to skin them is not only difficult but often results in the flesh being damaged.

2 sole weighing about 450g/1lb each   Butter

For the sauce
75gm/3oz butter   Juice of 1 lemon
Pinch of crunchy sea salt   Handful of parsley, chopped

This is exactly the same method as for the previous sole recipe, less the shrimps, of course. Place the sole on a grill or roasting tray and spread liberally with softened butter and pop under a pre-heated grill for 6-7 minutes until the skin starts to crisp and the butter becomes golden. Then place in a hot oven for a further 6-7 minutes to finish cooking.

While the sole is in the oven place the butter in a pan over a gentle heat, melting it until it starts to foam. You will notice it start to turn a light brown colour and begin to smell nutty. You have made *noissette* butter! At this stage remove from the heat, add the sea salt, and squeeze the lemon. Be very careful as this will spit and steam when the cold lemon juice mixes with the butter. Add the chopped parsley, which will further crackle and spit. Have a taste – it should be sharp and fresh tasting and non-oily. Place the whole fish on the plate and spoon 2-3 tablespoons of your butter over the back of the fish.

Serves 2

Try this too...

Once you have mastered making a good *noissette* butter you will find that it works virtually with anything except oily fish such as mackerel, herring and tuna. Perfect for the next time you need something quick and colourful to spoon over roasted cod, skate, scallops, or even a bowlful of grilled prawns.

Fried Sprats with Bread and a Lemon Wedge

Sprats were my grandmother's favourite and every Friday during the season you could guarantee what was for supper – a huge plate of sprats dredged in flour and lightly fried served with nothing more than a wedge of lemon and lightly buttered brown bread. I suppose, in a way, it is our English version of *Fritto Misto* (see page 153).

As many sprats as you think you can
   eat per person
Flour
Oil for frying

A few wedges of lemon
Sprinkling of sea salt
Brown bread

Dredge all of the sprats in flour and set aside ready for frying. In a frying pan, heat some vegetable oil until hot and add the sprats one at a time being careful not to overcrowd the pan. Fry until crisp on one side, then turn them over. Remove from the pan and drain on kitchen paper and continue with the remaining sprats. Serve them in a pile on a plate with the lemon wedges, a sprinkle of sea salt and brown bread.

Grilled Squid with Lemon, Garlic and Cumin

If you are cooking squid I insist that you do not substitute frozen for fresh. The frozen variety is from other parts of the world where the freezing process toughens the flesh and detracts from what is a fantastic eating experience. Once you have found a fishmonger selling fresh squid check that it is pure white, with no traces of pink on the flesh at all – this is the colour it turns after a few days. I find small and medium squid the best, however, a chunk of a large fresh squid can be equally as good and will not be tough as long as it is fresh. Squid is easy to prepare, and if you have a good fishmonger he will do it for you. But if you wish to tackle it yourself just hold the body in one hand and the tentacles in the other, give it a gentle tug and then put your fingers inside the body and feel around for the 'plastic quill' which is the bone. You can gently pull this out and then wash the body thoroughly to remove any gut which may be left inside. A tip here is to cut the first 5mm/¼" off the pointed end of the body and then run the squid body under the tap so that the water runs freely through it. This will flush out any grit or debris which may be left inside the body. Don't throw the tentacles away, cut them off just below the eyes of the squid and discard everything else. Give them a wash. Squid is great barbecued, doused in flour and quick fried, or, as in this dish, cooked on a grill plate after being marinated for a few hours.

4 squid weighing about 250g/9oz each, cleaned

Zest of 1 lemon

Good pinch of cumin

Pinch of sea salt

Good olive oil

1 clove of garlic, pasted

Juice of 1 lemon

½ handful of fresh coriander, chopped

Take the prepared squid, make a cut down one side of the body tube and open it out. If you have had to use chunks of a large squid then just lightly score the inside of the flesh which will help tenderise it. Mix together the lemon zest, cumin, sea salt, garlic and olive oil and rub into the squid and leave to marinate for a minimum of 2 hours in the fridge.

Heat your grill plate until white patches start to appear. Remove the squid from the marinade and grill either side for no more than 2 minutes to ensure that you get those lovely black grill lines across the flesh. Push the squid down with the back of a fish slice and do the same with the tentacles. Take the squid off the hot grill and serve on a plate with a sprinkling of sea salt, the juice of the lemon and a sprinkling of fresh chopped coriander. Serve with a mixed green salad.

Serves 4

Try this too...

Squid can be marinated in all sorts of simple marinades before grilling. Try fennel, chilli, sea salt and olive oil; or garlic, fresh thyme springs, sea salt and olive oil; or perhaps dried oregano, garlic, lemon juice and sea salt.

Deep-fried Squid with Sea Salt and Lemon

This is a far cry from the battered 'Rubber Rings' we so commonly find. If you don't like deep frying then lightly fry in a little oilve oil and add garlic, chilli and parsley; it won't be crisp but will be as good.

4 squid weighing about 250g/9oz each, cleaned	Lemon
Oil for deep frying	Sea salt

Follow the rules for buying and preparing squid as described on the previous page.

Dust the squid in seasoned flour and drop into a hot deep fat fryer at 325°F/170°C. Allow to cook for 3-4 minutes and drain on kitchen paper. Sprinkle with sea salt and a squeeze of lemon and serve – see how simple it is?

Serves 4

Try this too...

Add a little chopped garlic to the flour or some chilli or crushed Schezuan peppercorns. Try cornflour instead of plain flour as it gives a firmer, crisper coating.

Grilled Squid with Thyme Leaf and Garlic

This dish is incredibly simple, the cooking time is 3-4 minutes so it's ideal for that quick supper or perfect for a summer alfresco lunch. As always, it relies on good fresh squid, frozen will be too tough and you won't get that wonderful soft texture or subtle flavour, so it's worth waiting until your fishmonger has some pure white fresh local squid on the counter.

1 clove of garlic, crushed to a fine paste
Handful of fresh thyme sprigs
1 tsp lemon zest
Olive oil

4 medium-sized squid (about 175g/6oz each, cleaned and the body opened out)
Sea salt
Lemon juice

Place the garlic, thyme, lemon zest and olive oil in a bowl and mix together. Marinate the squid, including the tentacles, in the mixture for about 30 minutes.

Get a ribbed grill pan really hot on top of the stove and grill the squid for about 2 minutes either side, pressing down with a fish slice to give nice charred lines. Remove from the grill and place to one side on a plate, sprinkle with sea salt, a squeeze of lemon and then garnish with a small rocket salad dressed with lemon juice and olive oil.

Serves 4

Paparadelle with Grilled Swordfish, Wild Mushrooms and Oregano

Pasta and fish are always popular, whether it be a dish of simply steamed clams with spaghetti or a bowl of well-flavoured fresh herb pasta served as an accompaniment. In this recipe, swordfish, which can stand stronger flavours, is thinly sliced and chargrilled and served in a creamy, earthy, mushroom sauce with the fresh pungency of oregano bringing a real Mediterranean flavour. I really enjoy the texture of paparadelle, but you can use any pasta, the choice is yours.

250g/9oz paparadelle
Handful of dried porcini mushrooms
1 clove of garlic
Handful of fresh wild mushrooms (firm chestnut
  mushrooms cut into quarters also work well)
150ml/5fl oz cream

Handful of fresh oregano
400g/14oz swordfish, thinly sliced
150ml/5fl oz olive oil
Sea salt and black pepper
Parmesan

First cook the pasta in salted water until *al dente*, then rinse and set aside to cool until needed.

Soak the dried porcini mushrooms in 4-5 tablespoons of warm water for 30-40 minutes.

In a saucepan gently sweat the garlic and add the dried mushrooms and their juices. Bring to the boil and reduce by half. Add the fresh mushrooms, the cream and half the oregano and simmer for 2-3 minutes.

Meanwhile, lightly oil the swordfish and grill on a hot grill plate or barbecue for 1-2 minutes either side. Toss the sauce with the pasta, add the pieces of swordfish and the remaining oregano, fold it together gently and serve in big bowls with plenty of black pepper, some cut lemons and a little Parmesan.

Serves 4

Baked Swordfish with Rosemary and Garlic

If you want bags of flavour in a hurry then this simple recipe delivers the goods. You only need an oven, some good swordfish, about 10 minutes and you will serve up a fine dish. Baking swordfish rather than grilling it gives a better texture – juicier and softer. Just try it.

2 x 150g/5oz fresh swordfish steaks
Good olive oil, plenty
2 cloves of garlic, crushed to a paste

Handful of rosemary branches
Squeeze of lemon juice
Pinch of sea salt

Pre-heat your oven to 400°F/200°C/gas mark 6.

Place the swordfish steak in a roasting dish.

In a small saucepan gently warm the oil, garlic and rosemary to get those flavours infused in the oil. Do not allow it to get too hot. Taste the oil, the flavours should have come through. This is when it is ready. It shouldn't take more than 3-4 minutes.

Pour the oil over the swordfish and pop in the oven for 6-7 minutes. Then just add a squeeze of lemon, a sprinkling of sea salt and serve with a crisp green salad dressed with lemon and olive oil.

Serves 2

Grilled Trout with Cucumber and Mint

I went off trout a couple of years ago as I always seemed to be presented with the mass, weird commercial varieties which were commonly available. I found them too muddy and fatty. I have since, however, found a lovely source of brown trout. I have also enjoyed lake-caught trout which have been given to me by friends. During the summer a lightly grilled or pan-fried trout with a fresh clean cucumber and mint salad can reach perfection.

2 trout, weighing about 350g/12oz each,
   gutted but head on or off as you prefer
Butter for grilling the trout
1/2 cucumber, core removed and finely diced

Pinch of crunchy sea salt
1 tbsp fresh mint leaves, chopped
Squeeze of lime

Lightly brush the trout with butter and sprinkle with sea salt. Place under a pre-heated grill or on a barbecue grill for 5-6 minutes either side.

To make the salad, simply mix together the cucumber and mint and the sea salt and serve on a plate alongside the grilled trout – simple and summery.

Serves 2

Crisp-fried Tuna
with Pak Choi and Chilli Coconut Broth

I admit that a little work is involved in rolling the tuna but the rest of this recipe is really easy. It is packed with clean, fresh, Thai flavours. The pastry is crisp, concealing the warm tuna, which looks great and tastes absolutely delicious. If you don't have any fresh Thai herbs available just use a good green curry paste.

2 sheets of spring roll or filo pastry
1 red chilli, deseeded and chopped
2 sticks of lemongrass, finely chopped
Piece of finely sliced ginger or galangal
2 pieces of tuna, cut into rectangles
   (120g/4oz each and about 2cm thick)
Beaten egg

1 tin of coconut milk
4 lime leaves, shredded
Dash of fish sauce
Pinch of caster sugar
2 limes
1 bunch of pak choi
Handful of coriander leaves

Lay out the pastry in sheets. Fold in the two side edges about 10mm/½". Sprinkle liberally with some chopped chilli, lemon grass and ginger. Lay the tuna across the pastry, then turn the folded edges over the tuna. Roll the whole thing up from one end and then seal the pastry parcel with beaten egg. Your parcel should now look like a spring roll. Repeat and chill both rolls for 10 minutes before cooking.

To make the broth, place the rest of the ingredients (with the exception of the pak choi, coriander and lime juice) in a pan and bring to a simmer on a gentle heat. Remove the pan from the heat and leave to infuse for 10 minutes. Heat a deep fat fryer to 375°F/190°C/gas mark 5 and fry the tuna rolls until the pastry is crisp, about 4 minutes, remove and drain. To finish the broth, add the coriander, juice of 2 limes and the pak choi to the pan. Return to the heat and simmer for 2-3 minutes.

To serve the dish, pour the broth in a bowl, slice the tuna at an angle and rest it on top of the pak choi in the broth.

Serves 2

Grilled Tuna with Aubergine, Olives and Garlic

This is a really simple dish, ideal for a quick supper. I have left it plain, as the flavour of the smokey, salty aubergine is delicious with a good grilled slab of tuna. When cooking this at home I like to accompany it with a simple Greek salad. Just mix together red onion, cos lettuce leaves, tomatoes, fresh thyme leaf, good Feta cheese, olive oil and white wine vinegar. Dried oregano also works well in the dressing. The aubergine paste can be made up in advance and kept for 3-4 days and is equally delicious just spread on fresh hot toast.

1 aubergine	2 x 150gm/5oz tuna (choose nice bright red tuna
1 clove of garlic	as opposed to a dull brown)
1 tbsp black pitted olives	2 handfuls of good quality rocket leaves
150ml/5fl oz good fruity olive oil	dressed in lemon juice and oil
Handful of coriander, chopped	Lemon juice

Roast the aubergine whole in a low oven for 1-2 hours until soft. It will look almost deflated. Allow to cool and then peel.

Place the aubergine flesh in a food processor with the garlic and olives and pulse to a paste. Slowly drizzle in enough olive oil to form a smooth emulsion and then add the coriander.

To cook the tuna, brush it with olive oil and season and place on a pre-heated grill pan. Allow 1–2 minutes each side then remove and place on a plate. Top with the aubergine, a squeeze of lemon juice and finally the rocket leaves.

Serves 2

Grilled Tuna with Anchovy and Potato Salad

Far removed from the canned variety, the experience of eating fresh tuna is delicious and addictive. Tuna is ideal for those nervous about bones (as it doesn't have any) and for those who favour meat, as its 'rare' cooked appearance and texture make it an ideal introduction to seafood.

The secret of cooking tuna is to sear it on a high heat for a short period and then allow the fish a short period of rest. This will give the outside of the steak a firm texture, whilst the inside remains moist and rare. As with most fish, simple complementary flavours work well. This dish is no exception to that rule, with the creamy mayonnaise and nutty potatoes combining with the salty little anchovies and clean, fresh basil.

2 fresh tuna steaks, about 150g/5oz each
Olive oil
Sea salt
200g/7oz new potatoes
Jar of salted anchovies

Handful of fresh basil leaves
Dollop of mayonnaise (see page 37)
Juice of 1 lemon
Salad leaves (such as rocket, watercress)

Pre-heat a grill pan until it's very hot. Lightly oil the tuna on both sides and season sparingly with sea salt. Place the tuna onto the grill pan for 2 minutes each side and then rest the tuna steaks for a further 1-2 minutes.

To build the salad, mix together the potatoes, anchovies, basil, mayonnaise and lemon juice. Arrange this creation in the centre of the plate and then place the salad leaves on top.

The final step to a fabulous supper is to balance the tuna steak on top of the towering salad and drizzle it with olive oil and a final squeeze of lemon or lime juice. Then tuck in.

Serves 2

Charred Tuna with Roasted Pepper, Garlic and Thyme

Widely eaten around the Mediterranean, tuna is a prized fish, which has its own individual characteristic. When cooked properly its firm texture can be a delight, however, overcook it and it can be like eating a flannel. Because of its oil-rich tasty flesh there is so much that can be done with it. Firstly, you must choose a good piece of tuna. Avoid anything which is dark brown in colour; this indicates the fish hasn't been bled properly when caught and will have a slightly metallic taste. Instead, look for deep redness in colour and a firm touch.

If you are in your fishmonger's and you see bluefin tuna, buy it, regardless of cost, as this is the most delicious of all. You are, however, most likely to see yellow fin tuna which is more widely available in this country. I have found the best cut is a steak about 25mm/1" thick, cut from a loin. Allow the weight of the whole portion to be 150g-175g/5-6oz.

In this recipe the fish is charred on the grill pan and served with roasted peppers, garlic and thyme. The flavours are bold but the combination is perfect. If the tuna is cooked just so, you will enjoy a fine meal. I find tuna at its best cooked over a charcoal or wood-burning barbecue.

1 red pepper	2 cloves of garlic, pasted
1 yellow pepper	4 sprigs of thyme or rosemary
1 green pepper	4 x 200g/7oz tuna steaks, 25mm/1" thick
150ml/5fl oz olive oil	Lemon juice

In order to get the full sweetness from the peppers I like to skin them. To do this, grill, roast or turn them over an open flame until the skin blackens. If you are doing this over a barbecue or wood fire brush them well with the oil, allow the fire to flame and blacken the skin. When well blackened place them in a plastic bag and seal, and leave for about 10 minutes. Remove from the bag and scrape off the skin with the back of a knife. Slice the peppers roughly and set aside. Warm the oil with the garlic, herbs and olive oil and leave to infuse for a few minutes and then season.

Brush the tuna with oil and put it straight onto the grill. Allow it to cook for about 2 minutes each side. Allow to rest for 1 minute. You want the tuna to be just warm on the inside but still a deep red, thus keeping its flavour, texture and moisture. Don't be frightened of undercooking – tuna is superb eaten raw. To serve, put on a plate with the peppers and finish with a squeeze of lemon.

Serves 4

Fresh Grilled Tuna
with Anchovies, Lemon and Coriander

This is my absolute favourite way of cooking tuna. The little morsels of salty anchovies that appear in some mouthfuls and not others have pleasantly surprised everyone that I have cooked this dish for. The principal of larding the fish with these anchovies can work well with other fish. It works particularly well with monkfish, but substitute the coriander for sage.

Handful of coriander, finely chopped
8 anchovy fillets, salted if available
2 fresh tuna steaks, 175-200g/6-8 oz each

Lemon juice
Olive oil

Roll the anchovy fillets in the coriander, put on a tray and pop in the freezer overnight.

Stick the frozen anchovies into the tuna and snap off any remaining bits still visible. If you are short of time, simply make incisions in the tuna with a knife and push the anchovies in.

Brush with olive oil and cook on a grill plate or barbecue for 2 minutes either side. Finish with a sprinkling of sea salt and a squeeze of lemon and serve with a mixed salad.

Serves 2

Grilled Turbot with Beetroot and Cockle Salsa

I have used cockles in various dishes throughout this book. In this dish they add something wonderful to a lovely deep red-coloured salsa which works as a simple accompaniment to a luxurious grilled fillet of turbot. It would also work with almost any other fish. I have used fresh coriander as the favoured herb in this recipe but you could try using basil, tarragon or thyme. Try and get the largest turbot you can, taking your fillets from the top of the fish as this yields the fattest turbot. Ask your fishmonger to skin it for you.

2 fresh beetroot
450gm/1lb live cockles in their shells
Splash of white wine
Vegetable oil
4 fillets taken from as large a turbot as you
  can find, preferably from the top of the fish as
this yields the fattest fillet. Each fillet should
  weigh 150g/5oz. Ask your fishmonger to skin
  it for you
Lemon juice
Handful of coriander, chopped
Pinch of fresh horseradish, grated (optional)

Boil the beetroot until tender and then remove, cool and peel. Chop into small cubes about the size of your little fingernail. Add the cockles to a pan with a tight fitting lid, add a splash of wine and steam them open. Leave to cool and remove from the shells.

Heat some vegetable oil in a frying pan until smoking. Lay the turbot fillets on what would be the skin side down (you will know this side because it looks like it has wavy lines across it). Cook for 3-4 minutes until golden. Turn the fillets over and finish cooking for a further 3-4 minutes in a hot oven.

Finish the salsa by adding the cockles to the beetroot. Add a squeeze of lemon and half the chopped coriander, mix together and then place in a little pile in the centre of the plate. Add the remaining coriander to the juice from the cockles and spoon over the salsa and around the plate. When the fish is cooked, set it on the plate and sprinkle with a few more juices from the cockle pan.

Serves 4

Try this too...

Instead of using cockles use clams or mussels, and instead of the beetroot use chopped fennel or diced cucumber.

Braised Whelks with Coriander and Black Beans

At every one of our restaurants I always say to the other chefs and managers that it would be great for people to come to the counter and get their bowl of whelks or winkles and sit eating them in the window. All I ever get for this comment is 'people will never eat whelks, they're disgusting'. And so this has become a standing joke. I can understand why people think they don't like them. Perhaps they've only eaten them when they've been old and found them a bit chewy, rather than enjoying the small sweeter ones which are bite-sized. In any case, I decided to rise to the challenge and devise a recipe which included other flavours which would complement the humble whelk. So, if you want to prove to yourself that you've now become an adventurous fish cook, then give this one a try and see what the world thinks.

You can ask your fishmonger to cook the whelks, or, if you have them live, boil them in salted water for 10-12 minutes, then leave to cool. Remove from the shell with a crab pick by inserting it into the whelk and twisting it out of its shell.

1 kg/2¼ lb of freshly cooked whelks
Handful of coriander, chopped including the roots
1 clove of garlic, chopped
2 tbsp salted black beans
Piece of root ginger, 25mm/1" long, peeled

and finely grated
275ml/9 fl oz fish stock
1 tsp Thai fish sauce
2 handfuls of fine noodles
Juice of 1 lime

First wash the whelks to remove any grit and then finely slice.

In a heavy-based pan gently fry the garlic, onion, black beans and ginger till softened and then add the fish stock, fish sauce, whelks and half the coriander. Transfer to a casserole dish and place in a medium oven for 25-30 minutes.

While the whelks are braising, cook a couple of handfuls of fine noodles, drain and then place a handful into each serving bowl. Remove the dish from the oven, add the remaining coriander, the juice of a lime and pour over the noodles.

Serves 4

Fritto Misto

Means simply 'mixed fried' and that's just what it is.

The rule here is to use a little bit of everything. Try to include squid, small chunks of octopus, langoustines, maybe some razor clams, as well as fillets of fish such as red mullet, sardines or hake, or small whole fish such as anchovies, whitebait or small gurnard and bream. The fish are then lightly dusted in flour, fried in olive oil until golden and just served with a sprinkling of sea salt, chopped parsley and a squeeze of lemon juice.

Try this too...

If you have vegetarians coming to eat with you, or indeed just for a change, fry and serve small rounds of courgettes, courgette flowers, aubergines, fresh peas and thin potato slices in the same way. Instead of parsley, add fresh mint and maybe a little chopped chilli, good olive oil and perhaps a squeeze of lime juice.

Mixed Grilled Fish with Saffron and Garlic

This is like a *Fritto Misto* (see previous page) in the sense that you can use a bit of everything. In this recipe I have made it richer by glazing it with a Hollandaise Sauce (see page 35) and then spooning over some bright coloured well-flavoured garlic butter (see page 31) – it looks great.

You can try anything: hake fillet, scallops in the half-shell, mussels, prawns, salmon fillet, gurnard, pollock – almost anything which looks good on the day, except oily fish.

A mixture of fish (allow 150-175g/5-6oz
  per person)
Sea salt
275ml/9fl oz Hollandaise sauce

150g/5oz garlic butter
Pinch of saffron
Handful of fresh parsley, chopped
Juice of 1 lemon

Place all the fish and shellfish on a grill tray, lightly brush with oil and sprinkle with sea salt and grill for 6-7 minutes. This can be done on a grill pan or a barbecue.

Place the fish equally but randomly on each plate, coat each piece of fish with Hollandaise sauce, let some spill over the plate and in between the pieces. Put under a hot grill until the top is golden and glazed.

Lastly, melt the garlic butter in a pan, add the saffron, allow to infuse in the butter and then add the parsley. Spoon over the top of the fish and with a masterly flourish squeeze some lemon juice over each plate.

Serves 4

Fish Baked En Papillote

En papillote is a method of cooking fish wrapped in paper or foil and baked in the oven, usually with fresh herbs, garlic and wine. I have listed some options below and as this method of cooking is so easy no further explanation is needed. Great to bring to the table with the parcels still wrapped up so your guests can open them and enjoy the wonderful aromas and delicious flavours inside.

Sea Bream with Garlic and Thyme
Take one sea bream weighing about 350g/12oz per person. Make some slashes across the sides and place on to a sheet of foil or baking parchment big enough to wrap up the fish tightly. Add a splash of white wine, a knob of butter, a sprinkle of sea salt, one clove of garlic just bashed with a heavy knife, and a handful of fresh thyme. Then place on a roasting tray and bake in the oven for approximately 25 minutes on a high heat.

Salmon Steak with Fresh Dill and Lemon
Into the parcel place the salmon steaks, butter, some sea salt a chunk of lemon and some fresh dill and bake in a hot oven for 8-10 minutes.

Red Mullet with Oregano
Place one red mullet, weighing about 250g/9oz per person, some butter, a splash of white wine, some sea salt and a sprinkling of dried oregano into the parcel, and bake for 12-15 minutes.

Haddock with Mussels, Saffron and Clams
Place a chunk of haddock fillet, weighing about 150g/5oz, 3-4 mussels, a few clams or cockles, a pinch of saffron, some white wine and butter and a bashed clove of garlic into the parcel, and bake for 10-12 minutes.

Mixed Shellfish Bake
Into the parcel add a few clams and mussels, some fresh prawns, some previously boiled baby shore crabs, and some winkles with a handful of tarragon, a bashed clove of garlic, some white wine and a dash of double cream.

Taramasalata

Taramasalata: the roe of a cod lightly smoked and puréed with garlic, lemon juice and olive oil. That's all it is. But it is absolutely delicious and very far from the tubs you can buy in the supermarket. Find a good source of smoked cods' roe and make it yourself. You will love it. There are many recipes from different areas and families. I think this one works best.

2 slices of yesterday's bread
1 clove of garlic
Juice of 1 lemon

250g/9oz smoked cods' roe
200ml/7fl oz good olive oil

Put the bread and garlic into a food processor and whizz up until finely chopped. Then add the lemon juice to wet it down.

Put the cods' roe in with the skin still on – I think it adds to the smokey flavour. Continue to whizz until it is a fine paste and then in a steady stream pour in the olive oil until it starts to emulsify. If it gets too thick add a tablespoon or two of cold water. Taste and season, if necessary. Serve with black olives, pickled peppers and some pitta bread fresh off the grill.

Zuppa de Pescatore

I first cooked this dish after being inspired by a picture I had seen in a cook book a few years earlier. It looked fantastic and so appetising seeing a pan packed full of colour with all different kinds of seafood. I imagined the dish in the picture was exactly how local fishermen on small Mediterranean ports would eat it. I have since cooked it on a beach over a wood fire, on a family sailing holiday. I had no fish stock so I made do with seawater and wild herbs. It was great sitting round diving into the pan and spooning out the fresh cooked fish and shellfish. It can be as simple as this to make a meal become part of your memories.

Any selection of fish and shellfish can be used – lobster, clams, mussels, chunks of skate, steaks of hake, gurnard and cod, the choice is yours; buy enough to fill the pan packed tightly in one layer.

1 shallot, finely chopped	Selection of fish
2 cloves of garlic, chopped	570ml/1 pint fish stock
Olive oil	Sea salt
2 roasted tomatoes	Parsley or basil, chopped, for
Pinch of saffron	sprinkling over the top
3 or 4 sprigs of thyme	Grilled bread
Splash of Pernod	Aioli (see page 37)

In a large pan, sweat the shallots and garlic in the olive oil. Add the tomatoes, saffron and thyme and stir together. Add the Pernod and tip the pan away from you allowing it to catch fire and burn off the alcohol. Add the fish and cover with the fish stock. Simmer for 8-10 minutes.

Remove the thyme and season. Finally, sprinkle with fresh chopped herbs and accompany with grilled bread topped with the rich, garlicky aioli.

Serves 4

Fruits de Mer

In France, the eating of a *fruits de mer* is a national seaside pastime and a grand experience. Perfect for a long lunch, lots of wine and good conversation with old friends. There are no rules as to what you can put on a *fruits de mer*, you just simply use the best of what is available on the day. Apart from shellfish like crabs and lobsters, prawns, langoustines, winkles and whelks, everything is served raw. That includes oysters, clams, mussels and scallops. The only thing you have to make sure of is that the fish you are serving is very, very fresh.

Building a *Fruits de Mer*

The most impressive way to serve and present this grand dish is on a *fruits de mer* stand which can be bought from most kitchen shops. The stand is topped with a tray heaped with crushed ice, garnished with seaweed and the prepared shellfish piled in a mountain on top. Half the fun is seeing how big you can build it without it all falling off. Building good *fruits de mer* can become like a game of Jenga.

To prepare

Mussels, oysters and clams are all opened in the same way with an oyster knife, while lobsters are split in half, crabs have their top shell removed, their claws cracked and their bodies roughly chopped, and whelks, winkles and prawns are left whole. In France you may also find the addition of sea urchins: these are easily prepared by turning them upside down and cutting a hole in the top, draining off the juices to leave their beautiful orange coral on show. They are not easy to find in Britain but must be experienced if you come across them anywhere else.

To accompany the *Fruits de Mer*

Usually brown bread, olive oil, aioli, shallot vinegar (which is simply red wine vinegar mixed with lots of finely chopped shallots) and a bottle of Tabasco.

Fish and Shellfish with Thai Noodle Broth

I can still remember my first visit to a Thai restaurant and, much later in life, to Singapore. The first mouthful of green curry with lime leaves and galangal were flavours I had never experienced before. I found the cuisine exhilarating and, what's more, it is just so easy to recreate in the domestic kitchen. Just use the simple formula of fresh ingredients cooked together in proportion to suit your taste. Food in Singapore is such a huge part of culture and life. Markets open at 4am and people hungrily shop for the freshest crabs, lemongrass, prawns and coconuts and all that's best on display. When I first visited I found it hard shopping like this. I just had to buy everything. So it was crabs and ginger flowers for breakfast and steamed prawns and Thai basil over mid–morning coffee. In some ways this is how I want our FishWorks Seafood Cafés to be enjoyed. Just the sheer pleasure of first eating with your eyes from the magnificent display next to your table, then the chefs and waiters, giving everything a busy market feel, the guests amazed and enthralled, and spoilt for choice. But back to the dish which I first found being cooked and served at a fishing port in Singapore for the local fishermen sitting around at 3am after landing and grading their fish. A few prawns and noodles were their treat. Perhaps in a few years FishWorks will be seen as inland fish markets for everyone young and old to be amazed at and enjoy. The fish here are suggestions – buy a selection of what is fresh and what you fancy.

50mm/2" piece of ginger or galangal, peeled	12 mussels
2 cloves of garlic	8 clams
1 stick of lemongrass, chopped	4 raw prawns
1 tbsp fish sauce	4 scallops
1 hot chilli, whole	100g/4oz monkfish, cut into cubes
Bunch of fresh coriander, including the roots	1 sea bream, filleted and cut into pieces
6 fresh lime leaves	150g/5oz dried noodles
1 400ml/12fl oz tin of coconut milk	Juice of 2 limes

First make a paste by placing the ginger, garlic, lemongrass, fish sauce, chilli, the stems of the coriander, lime leaves and 4 tablespoons of coconut milk into a food processor and blend until a smooth paste is reached.

In a separate pan, steam open the mussels and clams in a little water. When opened, add the fish and shellfish and steam in the juices for 3-4 minutes. Add the curry paste. Stir gently and simmer for 2-3 minutes more before adding the remaining coconut milk and the juice of 1 lime. Bring to a gentle boil. Cook the noodles as per the instructions, drain thoroughly and place equally into 4 deep serving bowls. Pour the sauce over and spoon the fish around. Finish with the chopped coriander leaves and the rest of the lime juice.

Serves 4

Roasted Shellfish with Fennel and Chilli

This is one of the first dishes I cooked at the Seafood Café and was included in our first ever write-up in the *Which? Good Food Guide*. This recipe relies on a good selection of fresh shellfish and is not something you can plan in advance. A good variety of prime shellfish is essential to the dish.

2 cloves of garlic, pasted
Splash of Pernod
As much shellfish as you can eat per person:
   scallops, still in the half-shell, raw prawns,
   langoustines, winkles, whelks, mussels, clams,
   velvet crabs and razor clams

½ a fennel bulb
Pinch of dried chilli flakes
100g/4oz unsalted butter
Good handful of bronze fennel
1 mild red chilli, finely chopped
Juice of 1 lemon

Place the garlic and the Pernod into a saucepan with a tight fitting lid. Bring to the boil and allow the alcohol to evaporate. Add the mussels, cockles and clams and replace the lid. Cook for 3-4 minutes until the molluscs start to open. Discard any that stay shut, then set aside.

Onto a roasting tray put the finely chopped fennel bulb, the chilli flakes, the butter and the rest of the shellfish. Roast in a hot oven for 6-7 minutes. Remove from the oven. Pour the whole lot, including the valuable juices, into a mixing bowl. Add the contents of the pan with the molluscs in and using your hands mix it all together making sure everything is well coated.

Arrange into individual serving bowls and finish with a squeeze of lemon. Then armed with picks and crackers and a good chunk of bread, allow your guests to get stuck in.

Mixed Shellfish Marinière

If you walk into the fishmongers and are confronted with a good catch of shellfish then this is the recipe for you. Get a selection of what you can, cockles, mussels, clams, winkles, small whelks, velvet crabs – anything.

A good mix of shellfish (allow about 500g/1lb per person)

Splash of white wine

100g/4oz good homemade garlic butter (see page 31)

Handful of parsley, chopped

First, clean all the shellfish and place in a pan with a tight fitting lid. Add a splash of wine and steam until the shellfish have opened, discarding any that don't.

Divide the shellfish between 4 bowls. Melt the garlic butter and add to the juices. Throw in the parsley and then pour the wonderful green garlicky juices over the shellfish in each bowl.

Serves 1

Fresh Seafood Salad

The salad can be made and chilled a few hours in advance. On a hot day there is nothing to match it, piled into a bowl and topped with small salad shoots.

Splash of white wine
1 shallot, sliced
1 clove of garlic, chopped
12 large mussels
16 clams
100g/4oz monkfish fillet, cut into cubes
Langoustines, cooked

50g/2oz peeled prawns
Good olive oil
Handful of fresh tarragon or chervil, chopped
Handful of fresh flat parsley, chopped
Juice of 1 lemon
Sea salt
4 oysters, in the half-shell

Add a splash of wine to a large pan with a tight fitting lid. Add the garlic and shallot and simmer for 1 minute. Then add the clams and mussels and steam with the lid on until they have opened. When opened, remove them and leave to cool.

When cool, remove half of them from their shells. Add the monkfish to the remaining juices in the pan and poach for 3-4 minutes. If you need a bit more liquid, just add a splash of water before poaching.

Remove the monkfish and place in a bowl. Make the dressing by mixing together the oilve oil, herbs, lemon juice and sea salt and toss with the mussels, clams, prawns and langoustines. Chill for an hour and serve small piles on a plate or large bowl and finally top with an opened oyster and some salad shoots.

Serves 4

Try this too...

For an oriental-flavoured salad, use prawns and mussels and add beanshoots and dress with lime juice, ginger and coriander. For a fresh water taste use salmon, trout and crayfish and toss it together with lemon juice and dill or fennel.

Caesar Salad

Caesar salads are great, but they have to be just right. Fresh, green, sweet cos lettuce leaf, salty anchovies and a wonderful creamy dressing and crunchy – but not fatty – croûtons all topped with hard salty Parmesan shavings are essential.

1 large cos lettuce
10 anchovy fillets in oil
1 clove of garlic
1 tbsp mustard
1 egg yolk
1 tbsp Worcestershire sauce

50g/2oz Parmesan, shaved, using a potato
   peeler, into thin strips
100ml/4fl oz vegetable oil
100ml/4fl oz olive oil
Few tbsp cold water
Freshly made croûtons

First prepare the lettuce by cutting off the thick root, keeping the leaves whole and washing them thoroughly in cold water. Leave to drain and then place them in a large bowl ready for dressing.

In your food processor add 2 anchovy fillets, the clove of garlic, mustard, egg yolk, Worcestershire sauce and 3-4 shavings from the Parmesan. Whiz up this mixture to a smooth paste. Mix together the vegetable and olive oil – the vegetable oil will stop the olive oil being too fruity and dominant in the dressing. With the motor running, gradually add the mixed oils until you have a thick emulsion. Then add enough cold water to form bubbles within the dressing which will help lighten it.

Toss the lettuce leaves in the dressing, add the croûtons (thin slices of ciabata brushed with olive oil and placed in a hot oven until crisp, then rubbed with a garlic clove on both sides before being cut into bite-sized chunks) and Parmesan shavings. Serve.

Serves 4

Try this too...

Whilst Caesar dressing is fabulous on its own it also benefits from the addition of a fresh herb such as basil, coriander or parsley at the last minute. You then assemble the salad in the same way. For vegetarians, the anchovies can be left out and if you don't like the strong flavour of anchovies try topping the salad with freshly grilled sardine or mackerel fillets.

Fishcakes

Old-fashioned and delicious. A bit of mashed potato, a handful of fresh flavour and some fish, and you're there. They are good fun to make and you can create your own combinations. They are also great for children to make. The basic method is to mix cooked fish with the potato and some fresh herbs and salt and pepper to taste. I cook my fish in the oven wrapped in foil with a little olive oil and sea salt, and for smoked fish I poach it in milk with a bay leaf and maybe some cloves. The quantity of fish to potato is about 50/50. When it is cooked just mix it in with your hands after removing the skin and bones from the fish. Once the mix is made they can be shaped into any sized balls you like and then flattened, dusted in flour, dipped in beaten egg and breadcrumbs and then lighlty fried until crisp and maybe warmed in the oven if a bit of extra heat is needed. The best size is the one that suits you but I like them the size of crumpets. You can make them the day before, shape them and coat them ready for frying. Before serving, fry until golden then finish in the oven. The best way of telling they are warmed through is to poke your finger in the bottom. Serve it with the hole side down, no-one will notice, or use a thermometer. Following the above method I have listed some flavours for you to try.

Try this too...

Smoked Haddock and Chive
Poach smoked haddock with bay leaves in milk for about 6-7 minutes. Mix with potato, add some chives, shape and cook.

Cod and Parsley Leaf
Roast the cod in foil with a little olive oil and sea salt for about 7 minutes. Mix with the potato, a little anchovy essence and a handful of chopped parsley, sea salt and lemon juice. Shape and cook. Serve with tartare sauce or Mayonnaise (see page 37).

Asian Fishcakes
Make a paste from lemongrass, a splash of Thai fish sauce, some lime leaves, a teaspoon of ginger, a clove of garlic, half a mild chilli, the juice of one lime and a handful of coriander. Roast some white fish, cod or haddock or try pollack or gurnard as an alternative. Mix a few table-spoons of the Thai paste into the potato with the fish. Add more of the paste if you favour a more gutsy flavour. Shape and cook and serve with Chilli and Coriander Jam (see page 115). If you can't get to the shops and your store cupbord is bare then use a few tablespoons of readymade green or red curry paste, mixed with fresh coriander.

Tuna, Coriander and Lime
Roast some chunks of tuna in olive oil with a little sea salt. Mix into the potato with some fresh coriander, a dash of fish sauce and a squeeze of lime juice. Shape and cook.

Mussel, Leek and Saffron
Yes, shellfish are also good. Steam open some mussels, strain and cool, reserving the juice, and remove from the shells. Gently sweat some finely chopped leeks until softened, add a spoonful of the mussel juice and mix with the potato and add a handful of chopped tarragon. Shape and cook and serve with a rich garlicky Aioli (see page 37). Try using cockles instead or add a pinch of curry powder to the leeks for an extra twist.

FishWorks
Seafood Café
Cookbook

The Desserts

This book is primarily about fish. But, of course, nothing beats a really well-made dessert to round off a great meal. At our restaurants we have just a few regular favourites that we rotate throughout the year. They are classic, work wonderfully and everybody with a sweet tooth adores them.

As with the rest of the recipes in this book, they are simple to make and great to eat.

Sweet Pastry, Baking Blind and Pastry Cases

A few of our desserts are based on tart cases made with sweet pastry. I am not a natural dessert chef and always find making pastry fiddly. I am just too impatient. But good pastry is well worth mastering. This is the basic mix we use and the basic method for blind baking, (when the pastry is pre-cooked without a filling). This is done by making the pastry, lining a tart case with it and then lining the inside with greaseproof paper and filling it with dried beans or rice. This serves the purpose of holding it in place and prevents shrinking when cooking. It is then removed before filling.

250g/9oz soft butter	3 eggs
250g/9oz caster sugar	500g/1lb flour

Cream the butter and sugar in a mixer then add the eggs one at a time, then mix in the flour. This whole process should be completed as quickly as possible so as not to overwork the pastry. Roll the pastry into a tube or ball and wrap in Clingfilm and place into a fridge and rest for at least 1 hour. Roll out the pastry and line your baking tin. Return to the fridge for a further 20 minutes to prevent shrinkage. Line the pastry case with parchment paper and fill with baking or dried beans and bake for 15-20 minutes at 350°F/180°C/gas mark4. This is baking blind. Remove the baking beans and cook for a further 5 minutes to finish cooking the base of the pastry.

Makes 4 cases

White Chocolate and Coconut Mousse

This is a really light mousse. It tastes just like an ice-cold Bounty bar.

200ml/8fl oz milk	150g/5oz cream of coconut, grated
2 vanilla pods	150ml/5fl oz coconut milk
3 egg yolks	400g/14oz white chocolate
50g/2oz sugar	570ml/1 pint cream, lightly whipped
25g/1oz flour	

Boil the milk with the vanilla. Whisk the egg yolks with the sugar, add flour and then whisk in the heated milk. Sieve into another pan and bring to the boil stirring all the time. Cool slightly. Dissolve the grated coconut in the coconut milk by warming very gently, once dissolved add the white chocolate and mix well and allow to cool. Fold the chocolate and coconut into the pastry custard then lightly fold in the whipped cream. Put the mousse into serving bowls and place in the fridge for at least 3 hours before serving.

Serves 6

Crème Brûlée

I am very proud of our crème brûlées at FishWorks. This recipe works really well and to get a good one is fantastic. Get a bad one and you know it after the first mouthful.

500ml/18fl oz double cream
1 vanilla pod, split lengthways
4 egg yolks

50g/2oz caster sugar
A sprinkle of demerara sugar, to serve

Bring the cream and split vanilla pods to just below the boil and then remove from the heat and allow to infuse for 3-4 minutes. Whisk the egg yolks and sugar well and add the cream. Give it a thorough mix. Pass the mixture through a fine sieve, then pour into ramekins or, ideally, small flat dishes with a low rim. Bake in a low oven about 250-275°F/130-140°C/gas mark 1 for approximately 20 minutes or until just set. Allow to cool, then refrigerate for at least 2 hours before using. To serve sprinkle the top of the brûleé with demerara sugar then tip off the excess. Burn with a blowtorch or under a very hot grill until the sugar sets hard.

Serves 4

Peach Melba

The oldies are the best. Every Fortes café in Weston-super-Mare used to serve these back in the seventies – what a treat.

850ml/1½ pints water
800g/13/4lb caster sugar
150ml/5fl oz dessert wine
1 vanilla pod

6 ripe peaches, halved and stoned
200g/7oz fresh raspberries
6 scoops of best quality vanilla ice cream

Bring the water, sugar, wine and split vanilla pod to a gentle boil. Gently place the peaches in the syrup and poach for 5-10 minutes (the timing depends on the ripeness of the fruit). Gently remove the fruit with a slotted spoon; they should be firm but tender. Allow to cool, then peel away the skin.

Pour approximately 150ml/5fl oz of the water, sugar and wine mixture into a clean pan and add the raspberries and cook briefly for 2 minutes. Remove the raspberries from the syrup and blend in a food processor. Add some of the syrup, if necessary, to sweeten. To serve, place 2 halves of peach in a bowl, top with a scoop of vanilla ice cream and a couple of spoons of the raspberry syrup.

Makes 6

Fresh Lemon Tart

This is a perfect ending to a good meal.

4 lemons

9 eggs

375g/13oz caster sugar

300ml/10fl oz double cream

A 30cm/12" tart case lined with sweet pastry
   and blind-baked

Wash the lemons and zest them. Squeeze the juice and reserve. Beat the eggs and sugar until well blended and smooth. Add the cream and mix lightly. Add the lemon juice and zest and pour into your pastry case. Bake for 40 minutes at 275°F/140°C/gas mark 2.

Makes 1 tart

Sticky Toffee Pudding

This must be the nation's favourite pudding. Nearly every food supplier does one and every pub up and down the land owned by a chain serves it. Nothing beats a homemade one though and it is a great finish to a lazy Sunday lunch of fish stew or monkfish roast.

110g/4oz unsalted butter

325g/12oz dark muscavado sugar

130ml/4fl oz golden syrup

130ml/4fl oz black treacle

4 eggs

650ml/1¼ pint water

400g/14oz pitted dates

2 tbsp bicarbonate of soda

400g/14oz self-raising flour

For the sauce

1 litre/1¾ pints double cream

450g/1lb unsalted butter

450g/1lb muscavado sugar

Golden syrup

Black treacle

Cream together the butter, sugar, golden syrup and treacle. Beat in the eggs one at a time.

Boil the dates in the water and pour into a food processor. Whiz until roughly chopped. Add the bicarbonate of soda. Fold half the date mixture and half the flour into the egg mixture. Repeat with the remaining flour and date mix. Pour the mixture into a roasting tray or terrine lined with silicon paper. Bake in an oven at 400°F/200°C/gas mark 6 for 25 minutes.

For the sauce, boil the cream, butter and sugar and add treacle and golden syrup to taste.

Makes 1 tray

Rhubarb Fool

Until recently I had always had rhubarb fool made with custard. In this recipe it is made with mascarpone. I loved it when I first tasted it and now I insist on there being one on the dessert menu of all our restaurants. We change them with the seasons – in July we make a peach and raspberry fool which is brilliant.

1kg/2lb rhubarb, cut into 2"/25mm chunks	3 star anise
200ml/7fl oz orange juice	250g/9oz mascarpone
Zest of 1 orange	250ml/9fl oz double cream, softly whipped
300g/10oz caster sugar	2 tbsp icing sugar
1 vanilla pod	1 tsp vanilla essence

Begin by putting the rhubarb, orange juice and zest, the caster sugar, vanilla and star anise into a roasting tray and cover with foil. Bake for 20-25 minutes or until the rhubarb is tender. Remove from the oven and allow to cool. Drain off the syrup and reserve. Fold together the mascarpone, cream, sugar and vanilla essence. Mix some of the rhubarb into the cream, mixing well so the rhubarb breaks into thin strands and is even throughout.

Serves 6

Vanilla Ice Cream

Good ice cream makes a great dessert on its own and homemade is so much more luxurious than many shop-bought varieties, although Rocombe Farm and Hill Station, who make a wide range of flavours, are good. But once you start making your own you can make the basic custard and then substitute the vanilla for fresh fruit, coconut milk, ginger – anything you like.

500ml/18fl oz double cream	5 egg yolks
3 vanilla pods	150g/5oz caster sugar

Heat the double cream with the split vanilla pods to just below simmering then remove from the heat and allow to infuse for 10 minutes. Whisk the egg yolks and sugar and pour on the double cream. Return the mixture to a low heat and continue to stir all the time until the mixture has thickened and coats the back of a spoon. Be careful not to over-heat the mixture or to let it catch on the bottom of the pan. As soon as the custard is ready, remove it from the pan and allow to cool before freezing in an ice cream machine. If no ice cream machine is available, the next best method is to pour the mixture into a Tupperware container, and then place in the freezer returning every 30-45 minutes to beat the mixture to prevent ice crystals forming.

Serves 6

Chocolate Brownies

This is Matthew Prouse's recipe for chocolate brownies. He is our brilliant head chef at our Bristol restaurant. A hot squidgy tray of these straight from the oven doesn't last long as no one can resist pinching a bit when they walk past, which drives him mad! At FishWorks we serve them with our coffee, a perfect sticky end to a healthy seafood lunch.

275g/10oz unsalted butter
115g/4oz cocoa powder
4 eggs
450g/1lb caster sugar
115g/4oz plain flour

2 tsp vanilla essence
115g/4oz hazelnuts (roasted, skinned and
   roughly crushed)
225g/8oz plain chocolate chips

Melt the butter with the cocoa powder. Beat the eggs with the sugar and then mix in the butter. Add the flour, vanilla, nuts and chocolate chips. Pour the mixture into two Swiss roll tins lined with silicon paper and cook in an oven for 15-20 minutes at 350°F/180°C/gas mark 4. Allow to cool slightly then cut into small triangles or squares.

Makes 1 tray

Chocolate Tart

A really rich chocolatey tart, which can be made better by a dollop of clotted cream, served alongside. The secret is to buy good quality chocolate.

325g/12oz good quality dark chocolate
225g/8oz unsalted butter
6 egg yolks

4 whole eggs
75g/3oz caster sugar
A 12"/30cm tart case blind-baked

Melt the chocolate and butter over a pan of simmering water.

Whisk the eggs and sugar until very light and fluffy. Fold the chocolate mixture into the eggs and pour into the tart case. Bake at 350°F/180°C/gas mark 4 for 10 minutes.

Remove the tart from the oven and cool slightly before serving.

Makes 1 tart

Wines

I read a quote once which I thought was fun, 'Fish should swim three times: once in water, then in butter and last of all in good wine.' Whoever wrote it wasn't far wrong.

Wine used to be a mystery to me. The flowery language with talk of gooseberries and blackcurrants, vanilla and honey finish seemed alien. So, although I was doing well at the drinking part, I felt that I needed some professional advice in order to compile a short but serious wine list for our restaurants. I enlisted the help of Tim McCloughlin-Green, a wine consultant who had been a sommelier but was now acting on behalf of many leading restaurants. Tim's honest passion and enthusiasm seemed to fit with the culture at FishWorks. Now he puts together our wine lists which manage to achieve a balance between quality and value. The wines that follow give you a flavour of the type of wines that we offer. In a sense, they are a snap-shot in time as our wines are always changing as supplies and vintages come and go and new areas are discovered. This is where we are now....

Sparkling and Champagne

Prosecco Nino Franco
Champagne Philipponnat

White Wines

(France)
Sauvignon de Touraine Premier Cuvée
Côtes de Gasgogne Domaine san de
   Guilhelm
Terraces de Guilhelm Viellies Vignes
Sauvignon Dominique Duclos
Casteras Chardonnay
Tendem Sauvignon Rousanne
Picpoul de Pinet
Muscadet La Calriette
Pouilly Fumé Domaine Dagueneau
Chablis Domaine Louis Moreau
Clairette du Languedoc Condamine Bertrand

(Italy)
Villa Tonino Inzolia
Col della Corte Marche Bianco Moncaro
Pinot Grigio Poggio al Bosco
Verdicchio Terre Cortesi Moncaro

(Spain)
Palacio de Bornos Rueda Superia

(Australia)
Witt's End Semillion Chardonnay
Hollick Chardonnay

(Chile)
Aresti Sauvignon Blanc
Aresti Chardonnay

(New Zealand)
Canterbury House Sauvignon Blanc

Red Wines

(France)
Chateau Fougère La Noble
Merlot Dominique Duclos
Beaujolais Villages Domaine Dubost
Tendem Merlot Syrah

(Italy)
Sangiovese Moncaro
Montalbano Cabernet Franc

(Australia)
Witt's End Mataro Grenache

(Chile)
Aresti Merlot

(Spain)
Prado Rey

Index